easy-to-use

CHRISTMAS
PROGRAMS

easy-to-use

CHRISTMAS PROGRAMS

Cora Vogel

BAKER BOOK HOUSE
Grand Rapids, Michigan 49506

Copyright 1986 by
Baker Book House Company

ISBN: 0-8010-9302-3

Printed in the United States of America

Contents

Preface

Each Advent season I marvel at the variety of programs which are given to celebrate the birthday of our Lord Jesus Christ. The old, old story becomes new in each enactment of those wonderful events which are the pivot of all history. For many years I have had a desire to capture some of the beauty and inspiration of these celebrations and share them with others. This book of programs is in part a fulfillment of that ideal.

The programs are especially written for the novice church school director or committee members who have little time for planning and preparing such presentations. Most of these programs require little rehearsal time and few props. They can also be an integral part of the Church school's instructional program during the Advent season. Within the various presentations there is abundant opportunity for variations and adaptations to fit individual group needs.

The talents of many people have gone into the writing of this book. My hope and prayer is that whatever program you choose to give, it will not only lead you back to Bethlehem and Calvary, but also help you see the beauty of the living Lord in the glitter and glow of the season's festivities. May you then look forward to the future coming of that bright and Morning Star whose birthday we celebrate.

Acknowledgments

I owe a special debt of gratitude to William Hendricks who invited me to co-author the *Handbook of Christmas Programs* published by Baker Book House in 1978. His gentle proddings also gave the impetus to this present book. I wish to thank my many friends and relatives who so generously contributed programs and those who gave the necessary encouragement to continue writing and bring the work to completion. I am especially grateful to Betty De Vries for all of her helpful suggestions and expertise in editing this volume.

PART ONE

Advent Programs

1

An Advent Celebration

The following Advent wreath celebration was planned and arranged by Barbara Klaassen for the Riverside Christian Reformed Church of Grand Rapids, Michigan, Christmas, 1985. Before the first Sunday of Advent a request is made to the congregation for families who would be willing to participate in the ceremony of lighting the candles. Each Sunday a different family leads the congregation in the Advent wreath celebration.

Lighting of the First Candle

First Child: The world was in darkness before Jesus came.

Second Child: One candle is lighted to tell us to get ready for something special.

Mother: This first week in Advent is the time for us to remember that long ago, before Jesus was born, the people were sad and lonely. They knew a little about God from the prophets, but they didn't know very much about him. The people were in great darkness.

Song: Come, Thou Long-expected Jesus *(Audience)*

> Come, thou long-expected Jesus;
>   Born to set thy people free;
> From our fears and sins release us;
>   Let us find our rest in thee.

Israel's strength and consolation,
  Hope of all the earth thou art;
Dear desire of every nation,
  Joy of every longing heart.

Born thy people to deliver,
  Born a Child and yet a King,
Born to reign in us forever,
  Now thy gracious kingdom bring.

By thine own eternal Spirit
  Rule in all our hearts alone;
By thine all-sufficient merit
  Raise us to thy glorious throne.
                                    Charles Wesley

Father: Prepare ye the way of the LORD, make straight in the desert a highway for our God. And there shall come forth a rod out of the stem of Jesse, and a Branch shall grow out of his roots: And the spirit of the LORD shall rest upon him, the spirit of wisdom and understanding, the spirit of counsel and might, the spirit of knowledge and of the fear of the LORD: And shall make him of quick understanding in the fear of the LORD: and he shall not judge after the sight of his eyes, neither reprove after the hearing of his ears: But with righteousness shall he judge the poor, and reprove with equity for the meek of the earth: and he shall smite the earth with the rod of his mouth, and with the breath of his lips shall he slay the wicked. And righteousness shall be the girdle of his loins, and faithfulness the girdle of his reins. The wolf also shall dwell with the lamb, and the leopard shall lie down with the kid; and the calf and the young lion and the fatling together; and a little child shall lead them. And the cow and the bear shall feed; their young ones shall lie down together: and the lion shall eat straw like the ox. (Isa. 40:3; 11:1–7)

Audience: Our Father which art in heaven, hallowed be thy name. Thy kingdom come. Thy will be done in earth, as it is in heaven. Give us this day our daily bread. And forgive us our debts, as we forgive our debtors. And lead us not into temptation, but deliver us from evil: For thine is the kingdom, and the power, and the glory forever.

Father: Grant, Lord, that as we light this candle today it will be a light shining in our lives guiding us to the Christ Child. Fill our hearts with love and strengthen our hands to work that we may be ready for the coming of our Lord Jesus Christ. Amen.

Family: The grace of our Lord Jesus Christ be with us all— now and evermore. Amen.

Lighting of the Second Candle

Child: Our King and Savior is drawing near. His name will be called Wonderful Counselor, Mighty God, Everlasting Father, Prince of Peace.

Mother: One candle is lit to tell us to get ready. Two candles are lit to remind us that long ago before Jesus was born, the people were waiting for God, somehow, to come right down to them on earth.

It's hard for us to realize what it was like before Jesus came to earth. We look forward to Christmas with joy. But the Old Testament tells us of the days when people were oppressed and the prophets' message of the coming Messiah was the only hope.

Song: O Come, O Come, Emmanuel *(Audience)*

O come, O come, Emmanuel,
And ransom captive Israel,
That mourns in lonely exile here
Until the Son of God appear.

Refrain:
Rejoice! Rejoice! Emmanuel shall come to thee, O Israel.

O come, thou branch of Jesse's stem,
Unto thine own, and rescue them!
From depths of hell thy people save,
And give them victory o'er the grave.

O come, thou Bright and Morning Star,
And bring us comfort from afar!
Dispel the shadows of the night,
And turn our darkness into light.

Anonymous Latin Hymn
Tr. John Mason Neale

Father: The people were in darkness until Jesus came to be the Light.

Comfort ye, comfort ye my people, saith your God. Speak ye comfortably to Jerusalem, and cry unto her, that her warfare is accomplished, that her iniquity is pardoned: for she hath received of the Lord's hand double for all her sins. The voice of him that crieth in the wilderness, Prepare ye the way of the Lord, make straight in the desert a highway for our God. Every valley shall be exalted, and every mountain and hill shall be made low: and the crooked shall be made straight, and the rough places plain: And the glory of the Lord shall be revealed, and all flesh shall see it together: for the mouth of the Lord hath spoken it. The voice said, Cry. And he said, What shall I cry? All flesh is grass, and all the goodliness thereof is as the flower of the field: The grass withereth, the flower fadeth: because the spirit of the Lord bloweth upon it: surely the people is grass. (Isa. 40:1–7)

Audience: Our Father which art in heaven, hallowed be thy name. Thy kingdom come. Thy will be done in earth, as it is in heaven. Give us this day our daily bread. And forgive us our debts, as we forgive our debtors. And lead us not into temptation, but deliver us from evil: For thine is the kingdom, and the power, and the glory forever.

Father: We pray, our Father, that as the family of God prepares for the birthday of Jesus, each member may have a very real experience of God's love. Fill our hearts with love for thee, we pray, so that all we do will be thy will; through Jesus Christ our Lord. Amen.

Family: The grace of our Lord Jesus Christ be with us all— now and evermore. Amen.

Lighting of the Third Candle

Mother: Watch ye therefore: for ye know not when the master of the house cometh, at even, or at midnight, or at the cockcrowing, or in the morning: Lest coming suddenly he find you sleeping. (Mark 13:35, 36)

First Child: One candle is lit telling us to get ready.

Second child: Two candles are lit reminding us that long ago people were waiting for God to come to them.

Third Child: Three candles are lit to remind us that we will be judged at the second coming of our Lord.

Mother: The Advent season, four weeks long, gives us time to prepare our hearts and minds for the coming of the Lord. Advent is a season for spiritual preparation. Sometimes we are so busy getting ready for feasts and presents that we miss the real meaning of Christmas. Advent is a season to be penitent; to cleanse our lives of the things that keep us apart from God.

Song: As With Gladness Men of Old *(Audience)*

> As with gladness men of old
> Did the guiding star behold;
> As with joy they hailed its light,
> Leading onward, beaming bright,
> So, most gracious Lord, may we
> Evermore be led to thee.

As with joyful steps they sped
To that lowly manger bed,
There to bend the knee before
Him whom heaven and earth adore;
So may we with willing feet
Ever seek thy mercy seat.

As they offered gifts most rare
At that manger rude and bare,
So may we with holy joy,
Pure and free from sin's alloy,
All our costliest treasures bring,
Christ, to thee, our heavenly King.

William C. Dix

Father: Repent for the kingdom of heaven is at hand.

And there shall be signs in the sun, and in the moon, and in the stars; and upon the earth distress of nations, with perplexity; the sea and the waves roaring; Men's hearts failing them for fear, and for looking after those things which are coming on the earth: for the powers of heaven shall be shaken. And then shall they see the Son of Man coming in a cloud with power and great glory. And when these things begin to come to pass, then look up, and lift up your heads; for your redemption draweth nigh. (Luke 21:25–28)

Audience: Our Father which art in heaven, hallowed be thy name. Thy kingdom come. Thy will be done in earth, as it is in heaven. Give us this day our daily bread. And forgive us our debts, as we forgive our debtors. And lead us not into temptation, but deliver us from evil: For thine is the kingdom, and the power, and the glory forever.

Father: Grant Lord, that as we light these candles our hearts may be cleansed of all things hurtful and that we may be filled with love and kindness and humility. Help us to prepare for thy coming, for the sake of thy Son, our Lord. Amen.

Family: The grace of our Lord Jesus Christ be with us all—
now and evermore. Amen.

Lighting of the Fourth Candle

Mother: And it shall be said in that day, Lo, this is our God,
we have waited for him, we will be glad and rejoice in his
salvation.

First Child: One candle lit tells us to get ready.

Second Child: Two candles lit show us that long ago people
were waiting for God to come to them on earth.

Third Child: Three candles lit remind us we will be judged.

Mother: Four candles lit say that the Lord is at hand. God's
people were living in expectation before Jesus was born.
They were sad and oppressed. They prayed for someone to
help them. And Jesus was born! In a lowly stable bed he
came. Common shepherds on the hillside saw a bright
light and followed it to the Christ Child. Sometimes we
don't recognize the most important thing in our lives; we
must look for the Light, and then we must go *toward* that
Light.

Song: While Shepherds Watched Their Flocks by Night
(Audience)

> While shepherds watched their flocks by night,
>   All seated on the ground,
> The angel of the Lord came down,
>   And glory shown around.
>
> "Fear not," said he, for mighty dread
>   Had seized their troubled mind,
> "Glad tidings of great joy I bring,
>   To you and all mankind.
>
> "To you, in David's town, this day
>   Is born of David's line,

The Savior, who is Christ the Lord;
　　And this shall be the sign:

"The heavenly Babe you there shall find
　　To human view displayed,
All meanly wrapped in swaddling bands,
　　And in a manger laid."

Thus spake the seraph, and forthwith
　　Appeared a shining throng
Of angels praising God, who thus
　　Addressed their joyful song:

"All glory be to God on high,
　　And to the earth be peace,
Good will henceforth, from heaven to men,
　　Begin and never cease!"

> Nahum Tate

Third Child:　God sent his only Son, as the baby Jesus, to grow up here on earth, for men and women and children to see him and to know him better.

Song:　Away In a Manger *(Audience)*

Away in a manger, no crib for His bed,
　　The little Lord Jesus lay down his sweet head;
The stars in the heavens looked down where he lay,
　　The little Lord Jesus asleep in the hay.

The cattle are lowing, the baby awakes,
　　But little Lord Jesus, no crying he makes;
I love thee, Lord Jesus, look down from the sky,
　　And stay by my cradle till morning is nigh.

Be near me, Lord Jesus! I ask thee to stay
　　Close by me forever, and love me, I pray.
Bless all the dear children in thy tender care.
　　And take us to heaven to live with thee there

> Anonymous

Father: And it came to pass in those days, that there went a decree from Caesar Augustus, that all the world should be taxed. (And this taxing was first made when Cyrenius was governor of Syria.) And all went to be taxed, every one into his own city. And Joseph also went up from Galilee, out of the city of David, which is called Bethlehem; (because he was of the house and lineage of David:) To be taxed with Mary his espoused wife, being great with child. And it was so, that, while they were there, the days were accomplished that she should be delivered. And she brought forth her firstborn son, and wrapped him in swaddling clothes, and laid him in a manger; because there was no room for them in the inn. And there were in the same country shepherds abiding in the field, keeping watch over their flock by night. And, lo, the angel of the Lord came upon them, and the glory of the Lord shone round about them: and they were sore afraid. And the angel said unto them, Fear not: for, behold, I bring you good tidings of great joy, which shall be to all people. For unto you is born this day in the city of David a Saviour, which is Christ the Lord. And this shall be a sign unto you; Ye shall find the babe wrapped in swaddling clothes, lying in a manger. And suddenly there was with the angel a multitude of the heavenly host praising God, and saying, Glory to God in the highest, and on earth peace, good will toward men. And it came to pass, as the angels were gone away from them into heaven, the shepherds said one to another, Let us now go even unto Bethlehem, and see this thing which is come to pass, which the Lord hath made known unto us. And they came with haste, and found Mary, and Joseph, and the babe lying in a manger. And when they had seen it, they made known abroad the saying which was told them concerning this child. (Luke 2:1–17)

Audience: Our Father which art in heaven, hallowed be thy name. Thy kingdom come. Thy will be done in earth, as it is in heaven. Give us this day our daily bread. And forgive us our debts, as we forgive our debtors. And lead us not into temptation, but deliver us from evil: For thine is the kingdom, and the power, and the glory forever.

Father: O God, who each year makes us glad with the expectation of Christmas, make our hearts ready for all Christmas joys; through Jesus Christ our Lord. Amen.

Family: The grace of our Lord Jesus Christ be with us all— now and evermore. Amen.

2

Chrismons
A Preparation for Advent

A chrismon is a monogram of Christ. Early Christians used them to identify one another and to escape persecution. They were also used as simple reminders of what Christ had done for them. Today chrismons are used to help Christians prepare for Advent. During the Advent season we see the monograms in various forms, such as banners, Christmas tree ornaments, designs for program covers, and drawings.

Teaching the meanings of the chrismons to the church school children can be an effective way to acquaint the entire congregation with their significance. The younger children could be given copies of the chrismons to cut out, color, and hang on the church Christmas tree. Some of the older classes could make bulletin covers, banners, or posters featuring the various chrismons. These can be used in the worship services as the leaders explain their meaning and the congregation joins in the adoration of Christ the Lord.

Patterns for Chrismons

CROWN

FISH

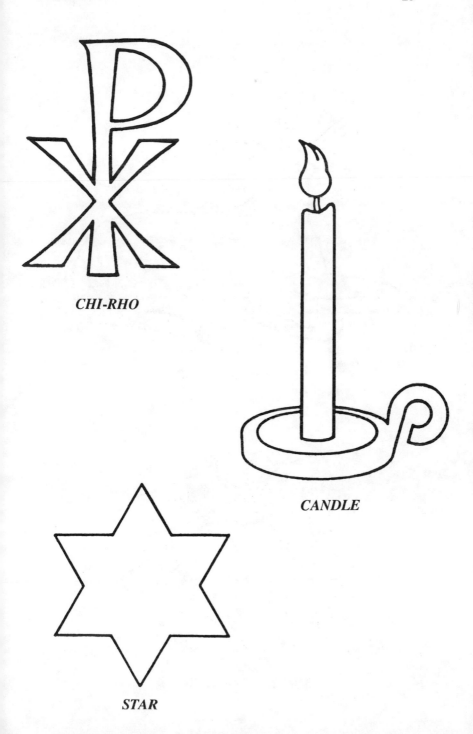

CHI-RHO

CANDLE

STAR

SUFFERING LAMB

VICTORIOUS LAMB

IHS

CIRCLE

ALPHA AND OMEGA

CORNERSTONE

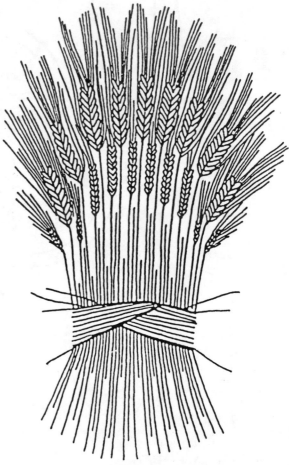

WHEAT

SUN OF RIGHTEOUSNESS

THE ANCHOR CROSS

ADVENT ROSE

Crown

Leader: One of the most familiar symbols in Christian art is the crown. It reminds Christians that Christ is King. When a crown is placed on the head of a human ruler, the crown stands for authority, royalty, power, dominion. As King of kings and Lord of lords, Jesus Christ has been given all authority, honor, wisdom, and might. In the Book of Revelation, John says that hosts of angels continually sing praise to Christ, worshiping the one who is seated at the right hand of God.

   Join me in worshiping Christ the King of glory reading responsively from the Revelation of John and singing his praise in the words of the hymnwriter.

Leader: And the four beasts had each of them six wings about him; and they were full of eyes within; and they rest not day and night saying,

Audience: Holy, holy, holy, Lord God Almighty, which was, and is, and is to come.

Leader: And when those beasts give glory and honor and thanks to him that sat on the throne, who liveth for ever and ever, the four and twenty elders fall down before him that sat on the throne, and worship him that liveth for ever and ever, and cast their crowns before the throne, saying,

Audience: Thou art worthy, O Lord, to receive glory and honor and power: for thou hast created all things, and for thy pleasure they are and were created.

Leader: And them that had gotten the victory over the beast, and over his image, and over his mark, and over the number of his name, stand on the sea of glass, having the harps of God. And they sing the song of Moses the servant of God, and the song of the Lamb, saying,

Audience: Great and marvelous are thy works, Lord God Almighty; just and true are thy ways, thou King of saints.

Who shall not fear thee, O Lord, and glorify thy name? for thou only art holy: for all nations shall come and worship before thee; for thy judgments are made manifest.

Scripture Readings: Revelation 4:8–11; 15:2b–4

Song: Crown Him with Many Crowns *(Audience)*

> Crown him with many crowns,
>   The Lamb upon his throne,
> Hark! how the heavenly anthem drowns
>   All music but its own.
> Awake! my soul and sing
>   Of him who died for thee;
> And hail him as thy matchless King
>   Through all eternity.
>
> Crown him the Lord of life:
>   Who triumphed o'er the grave,
> Who rose victorious in the strife
>   For those he came to save;
> His glories now we sing,
>   Who died and rose on high,
> Who died eternal life to bring,
>   And lives that death may die.
>
> Crown him the Lord of heaven:
>   One with the Father known,
> One with the Spirit through him given
>   From yonder glorious throne.
> To thee be endless praise,
>   For thou for us hast died;
> Be thou, O Lord, through endless days
>   Adored and magnified.
>   Matthew Bridges
>   Stanza 2 Godfrey Thring

Fish

Leader: Early Christians were cruelly persecuted for their faith. One way they avoided arrest was to use the fish symbol. When pagans painted a fish on their houses, that meant there was a funeral banquet inside. But when Christians displayed that symbol, it meant a worship service would be held that night.

Why did Christians use a fish as the sign of their faith? Because the Greek letters which happen to spell fish are the first letters of the five Greek words meaning "Jesus Christ, Son of God, Savior." In English those five first letters look something like this:

(Leader holds a poster board displaying these letters.)

I stands for the Greek word for Jesus

CH stands for the Greek word for Christ

TH stands for the Greek word for God

U stands for the Greek word for Son

S stands for the Greek word for Savior

ICHTHUS (pronounced ick-thoose)

This could be called the first creed. It is a simple but powerful statement of Christian belief. The apostle John in his first letter to the churches tells us that the foundation of our faith is God's great love for us shown through Jesus Christ our Lord and Savior. John also tells us what should be our response to God's wonderful love. Let us read responsively from 1 John 4:9–21:

Leader: In this was manifested the love of God toward us, because that God sent his only begotten Son into the world, that we might live through him.

Audience: Herein is love, not that we loved God, but that he loved us, and sent his Son to be the propitiation for our sins.

Leader: Beloved, if God so loved us, we ought also to love one another.

Audience: No man hath seen God at any time. If we love one another, God dwelleth in us, and his love is perfected in us.

Leader: Hereby know we that we dwell in him, and he in us, because he hath given us of his Spirit.

Audience: And we have seen and do testify that the Father sent the Son to be the Saviour of the world.

Leader: Whosoever shall confess that Jesus is the Son of God, God dwelleth in him, and he in God.

Audience: And we have known and believed the love that God hath to us. God is love; and he that dwelleth in love dwelleth in God, and God in him.

Leader: Herein is our love made perfect, that we may have boldness in the day of judgment: because as he is, so are we in this world.

Audience: There is no fear in love; but perfect love casteth out fear; because fear hath torment. He that feareth is not made perfect in love.

Leader: We love him, because he first loved us.

Audience: If a man say, I love God, and hateth his brother, he is a liar: for he that loveth not his brother whom he hath seen, how can he love God whom he hath not seen?

Leader: And this commandment have we from him, that he who loveth God love his brother also.

Song: What Wondrous Love *(Audience)*

> What wondrous love is this, O my soul, O my soul!
>   What wondrous love is this, O my soul!
> That caused the Lord of life to bear the heavy cross—
>   What wondrous love is this, O my soul!

What wondrous love is this, O my soul, O my soul!
  What wondrous love is this, O my soul!
That Christ should lay aside His crown for my soul—
  What wondrous love is this, O my soul!

And when from death I'm free, I'll sing on, I'll sing on,
  And when from death I'm free, I'll sing on;
And when from death I'm free, I'll sing and joyful be,
  And through eternity I'll sing on.

To God and to the lamb I will sing, I will sing,
  To God and to the lamb I will sing,
To God and to the lamb who is the great I AM,
  While millions join the theme, I will sing.

Traditional Southern Folk Hymn

Chi-Rho

Leader: The oldest monogram for Christ is the Chi-Rho. Most of the educated people in New Testament times spoke and wrote Greek. This monogram is formed by placing the Greek letters X (Chi, pronounced Ki—rhymes with hi) and P (Rho, pronounced row) together.

Long ago Constantine the Great, after his conversion to Christianity, put the Chi-Rho on the banners of his army as he marched against the Roman emperor, Maxentius.

X and P are the first two letters of the Greek word for Christ. When spelled in Greek capital letters, the word Christ looks like this:

(Leader holds up poster board displaying Greek word.)

ΧΡΙΣΤΟΣ

Join me in praising Christ the anointed One using the words of the writer to the Hebrews and of the apostle John in the Book of Revelation.

Leader: Thy throne, O God, is for ever and ever: a sceptre of righteousness is the sceptre of thy kingdom.

Audience: Thou hast loved righteousness, and hated iniquity; therefore God, even thy God, hath anointed thee with the oil of gladness above thy fellows.

Leader: And, Thou, Lord, in the beginning hast laid the foundation of the earth; and the heavens are the works of thine hands:

Audience: They shall perish; but thou remainest; and they all shall wax old as doth a garment; And as a vesture shalt thou fold them up, and they shall be changed: but thou art the same, and thy years shall not fail.

Leader: Grace be unto you, and peace, from him which is, and which was, and which is to come; and from the seven Spirits which are before his throne; And from Jesus Christ, who is the faithful witness, and the first begotten of the dead, and the prince of the kings of the earth.

Audience: Unto him that loved us, and washed us from our sins in his own blood, and hath made us kings and priests unto God and his Father; to him be glory, and dominion for ever and ever. Amen.

All: Behold, he cometh with clouds; and every eye shall see him, and they also which pierced him: and all kindreds of the earth shall wail because of him. Even so, Amen.

Scripture Readings: Hebrews 1:8–12; Revelation 1:4–7.

Song: Christ, Whose Glory Fills the Skies *(Audience)*

> Christ, whose glory fills the skies,
>   Christ, the true and only Light,
> Sun of Righteousness, arise,
>   Triumph o'er the shades of night;

Dayspring from on high, be near;
    Daystar, in my heart appear.

Dark and dismal is the morn
    Unaccompanied by thee;
Joyless is the day's return
    Till thy mercy's beams I see;
Till they inward light impart,
    Till thou cheer and warm my heart.

Visit, then, this soul of mine;
    Pierce the gloom of sin and grief;
Fill me, Radiancy Divine;
    Scatter all my unbelief;
More and more thyself display,
    Shining to the perfect day.

                                    Charles Wesley

Candle

Leader: When early Christians were persecuted by the Romans, they held services in dark, deep catacombs beneath the city. People were also buried in these catacombs, and often the bread and wine used for Communion were placed on top of a tomb. Since it was dark, candles were lighted so that the congregation could see. At first, candles simply served the same purpose as electric light bulbs—to give light for people to see.

However, a deeper significance was soon attached to the candles. The early Christians remembered the words of Jesus, "I am the light of the world." They knew Jesus had caused the light of truth to shine in their lives, giving them hope and courage. When candles were lit, Christians remembered Jesus as the "Light of the world."

Reader One: Isaiah foretold of Jesus coming to be the Light of the world: He said, "Arise, shine; for thy light is come, and the glory of the Lord is risen upon thee. For, behold, the darkness shall cover the earth, and gross darkness the people: but the Lord shall arise upon thee, and his glory shall be seen upon thee. And the Gentiles shall come to thy light, and kings to the brightness of thy rising. . . . The sun shall be no more thy light by day; neither for brightness shall the moon give light unto thee: but the LORD shall be unto thee an everlasting light, and thy God thy glory." (Isa. 60:1–3, 19)

Reader Two: In his Gospel John wrote about Jesus, the fulfillment of Isaiah's prophecy: "In the beginning was the Word, and the Word was with God, and the Word was God. The same was in the beginning with God. All things were made by him: and without him was not any thing made that was made. In him was life; and the life was the light of men. And the light shineth in darkness; and the darkness comprehended it not. There was a man sent from God, whose name was John. The same came for a witness, to bear witness of the Light, that all men through him might believe. He was not that Light, but was sent to bear witness of that Light. That was the true Light, which lighteth every man that cometh into the world." (John 1:1–9)

Reader Three: In the Book of Revelation John describes his vision of the new heaven and earth where God's people will one day live with Jesus, the Light of the world. He saw a beautiful city with the streets of gold and gates of precious jewels. He said, "And the city had no need of the sun, neither of the moon, to shine in it: for the glory of God did lighten it, and the Lamb is the light thereof. And the nations of them which are saved shall walk in the light of it: and the kings of the earth do bring their glory and honor into it. . . . And there shall be no night there; and they need no candle, neither light of the sun; for the Lord God giveth them light: and they shall reign for ever and ever." (Rev. 21:23–24; 22:5)

Song: The Light of the World Is Jesus (*Audience*)

The whole world was lost in the darkness of sin;
   The Light of the world is Jesus;
Like the sunshine at noonday His glory shone in,
   The Light of the world is Jesus.

Refrain:
Come to the Light, 'tis shining for thee;
   Sweetly the Light has dawned upon me;
Once I was blind, but now I can see;
   The Light of the world is Jesus.

No darkness have we who in Jesus abide,
   The Light of the world is Jesus;
We walk in the Light when we follow our Guide,
   The Light of the world is Jesus.

No need of the sunlight in heaven, we're told,
   The Light of the world is Jesus;
The Lamb is the Light in the City of Gold,
   The Light of the world is Jesus.

                                             P. B. Bliss

The Suffering Lamb

Leader: Long before Jesus was born, the prophet Isaiah wrote about the sufferings of one who would come to save Israel. In beautiful poetry he said that this redeemer would take the sins of his people on himself. Isaiah called him the "Suffering Servant" and compared his obedience to that of a lamb who goes quietly to be slaughtered.

John the Baptist told the Jews that Jesus was that Lamb. John said, "Behold, the Lamb of God who takes away the sins of the world."

A lamb is a good symbol of Jesus Christ. A lamb is always obedient to the shepherd. Jesus was obedient to God's will for his life as he prayed, "Not my will, but thine be done." Jesus, as the Lamb of God, is an offering to God for the sins of mankind. Jesus took our sins on himself as he suffered, died, and rose again.

The lamb in a lying down position portrays suffering. The suffering lamb is especially appropriate for our Communion celebration this Sunday in Advent. The three-rayed cloud surrounding the lamb's head is symbolic of divinity.

Reader One: All we like sheep have gone astray; we have turned every one to his own way; and the LORD hath laid on him the iniquity of us all. He was oppressed, and he was afflicted, yet he opened not his mouth: he is brought as a lamb to the slaughter, and as a sheep before her shearers is dumb, so he openeth not his mouth. He was taken from prison and from judgment: and who shall declare his generation? for he was cut off out of the land of the living: for the transgression of my people was he stricken. And he made his grave with the wicked, and with the rich in his death; because he had done no violence, neither was any deceit in his mouth. Yet it pleased the Lord to bruise him; he hath put him to grief: when thou shalt make his soul an offering for sin, he shall see his seed, he shall prolong his days, and the pleasure of the Lord shall prosper in his hand. (Isa. 53:6–10)

Reader Two: . . . John seeth Jesus coming unto him, and saith, Behold the Lamb of God, which taketh away the sin of the world. This is he of whom I said, After me cometh a man which is preferred before me: for he was before me. And I knew him not: but that he should be made manifest to Israel, Therefore am I come baptizing with water. And John bare record, saying, I saw the Spirit descending from heaven like a dove, and it abode upon him. And I knew him not: but he that sent me to baptize with water, the same said unto me, Upon whom thou shalt see the Spirit descending, and remaining on him, the same is he which baptizeth with the Holy Ghost. And I saw and bear record that this is the Son of God. (John 1:29–34)

Reader Three: But as he which hath called you is holy, so be ye holy in all manner of conversation; Because it is written, Be ye holy; for I am holy. And if ye call on the Father, who without respect of persons judgeth according to every man's work, pass the time of your sojourning here in fear: Forasmuch as ye know that ye were not redeemed with corruptible things, as silver and gold, from your vain conversation received by tradition from your fathers; But with the precious blood of Christ, as of a lamb without blemish and without spot: Who verily was foreordained before the foundation of the world, but was manifest in these last times for you, Who by him do believe in God, that raised him up from the dead, and gave him glory; that your faith and hope might be in God (1 Peter 1:15–21)

Song: Alas, And Did My Savior Bleed *(Audience)*

> Alas, and did my Savior bleed,
>   And did my sovereign die?
> Would he devote that sacred head
>   For sinners such as I?
>
> Was it for crimes that I have done
>   He groaned upon the tree?
> Amazing pity, grace unknown,
>   And love beyond degree!
>
> Well might the sun in darkness hide,
>   And shut his glories in,
> When Christ, the mighty Maker, died
>   For man, the creature's, sin.
>   Isaac Watts

Victorious Lamb

Reader One: The lamb, standing strong and proud, signifies Jesus' victory over death. The white banner always has a red cross on it. The staff which is shaped like a cross reminds us of Christ's death on the cross.

   In the Book of Revelation John tells of his vision of the victorious Lamb. Let us praise the Lamb together with

John's description of the heavenly hosts celebrating the Lamb's victory over sin, death and hell.

Reader Two: And I saw in the right hand of him that sat on the throne a book written within and on the backside, sealed with seven seals. And I saw a strong angel proclaiming with a loud voice, Who is worthy to open the book, and to loose the seals thereof? And no man in heaven, nor in earth, neither under the earth, was able to open the book, neither to look thereon. And I wept much, because no man was found worthy to open and to read the book, neither to look thereon. And one of the elders saith unto me, Weep not: behold, the Lion of the tribe of Juda, the Root of David, hath prevailed to open the book, and to loose the seven seals thereof. And I beheld, and, lo, in the midst of the throne and of the four beasts and in the midst of the elders, stood a Lamb as it had been slain, having seven horns and seven eyes, which are the seven Spirits of God sent forth into all the earth. And he came and took the book out of the right hand of him that sat on the throne. And when he had taken the book, the four beasts and four and twenty elders fell down before the Lamb, having every one of them harps, and golden vials full of odors, which are the prayers of saints.

Audience: And they sang a new song, saying, Thou art worthy to take the book, and to open the seals thereof: for thou wast slain, and hast redeemed us to God by thy blood out of every kindred, and tongue, and people, and nation; And hast made us unto our God kings and priests: and we shall reign on earth.

Reader One: And I beheld, and I heard the voice of many angels round about the throne and the beasts and the elders: and the number of them was ten thousand times ten thousand, and thousands of thousands; Saying with a loud voice,

Audience: Worthy is the Lamb that was slain to receive power, and riches, and wisdom, and strength, and honor, and glory, and blessing. And every creature which is in heaven, and on the earth, and under the earth, and such as are in the sea, and all that are in them, heard I saying, Blessing, and honor, and glory, and power, be unto him that sitteth upon the throne, and unto the Lamb for ever and ever.

Scripture Reading: Revelation 5:1–13.

Song: Hark! Ten Thousand Harps and Voices *(Audience)*

> Hark! ten thousand harps and voices
>   Sound the note of praise above;
> Jesus reigns, and heav'n rejoices;
>   Jesus reigns, the God of love.
> See, He sits while angels stand;
>   Jesus rules at God's right hand.

> Refrain:

> Alleluia! Alleluia! Alleluia! Amen.

> King of glory! reign forever,
>   Thine an everlasting crown;
> Nothing from thy love shall sever
>   Those whom Thou hast made Thine own;
> Happy objects of Thy grace
>   Destined to behold Thy face.

> Savior, hasten thine appearing;
>   Bring, O bring the glorious day,
> When, the awful summons hearing,
>   Heav'n and earth shall pass away;
> Then, with golden harps, we'll sing,
>   "Glory, glory to our king!"

> > Thomas Kelly

Star

Reader One: A six-pointed star is a good symbol for Christ because each point may be used to remind us of something of his nature: power, wisdom, majesty, love, mercy, and justice.

Long ago Balaam prophesied about the "star that would come out of Jacob."

> I shall see him, but not now: I shall behold him, but not nigh: there shall come a Star out of Jacob, and a Sceptre shall rise out of Israel, and shall smite the corners of Moab, and destroy all the children of Sheth. And Edom shall be a possession, Seir also shall be a possession for his enemies; and Israel shall do valiantly. Out of Jacob shall come he that shall have dominion, and shall destroy him that remaineth of the city.

Reader Two: Jesus Christ was that Star. Peter tells us in the first chapter of his second letter to pay attention to prophecy so the Day Star will rise in our hearts.

> We have also a more sure word of prophecy; whereunto ye do well that ye take heed, as unto a light that shineth in a dark place, until the day dawn, and the day star arise in your hearts: Knowing this first, that no prophecy of the scripture is of any private interpretation. For the prophecy came not in old time by the will of man: but holy men of God spake as they were moved by the Holy Ghost.

Reader Three: In the last chapter of the last book of the Bible Jesus speaks of himself as the "bright and morning star."

> And, behold, I come quickly; and my reward is with me, to give every man according as his work shall be. I am the Alpha and Omega, the beginning and the end, the first and the last. . . . I Jesus have sent mine angel to testify unto

you these things in the churches. I am the root and the offspring of David, and the bright and morning star. And the Spirit and the bride say, Come. And let him that heareth say, Come. And let him that is athirst come. And whosoever will, let him take the water of life freely. . . . He which testifieth these things saith, Surely I come quickly. Amen. Even so, come, Lord Jesus.

Scripture Readings: Numbers 24:17–19; 2 Peter 1:19–21; Revelation 22:12–13, 16–17, 20.

Song: How Bright Appears the Morning Star *(Audience)*

How bright appears the Morning Star,
With mercy beaming from afar;
    The host of heaven rejoices;
O Righteous Branch, O Jesse's Rod!
Thou Son of Man and Son of God!
    We, too, will lift our voices:
        Jesus, Jesus!
        Holy, holy, yet most lowly,
        Draw thou near us;
        Great Emmanuel, come and hear us.

Though circled by the hosts on high,
He deigned to cast a pitying eye
    Upon his helpless creature;
The whole creation's Head and Lord,
By highest seraphim adored,
    Assumed our very nature.
        Jesus, grant us,
        Through thy merit to inherit
        Thy salvation;
        Hear, O hear our supplication.

Rejoice, ye heavens; thou earth, reply;
With praise, ye sinners, fill the sky,
    For this His incarnation.
Incarnate God, put forth thy power,
Ride on, ride on, great Conqueror
    Till all know thy salvation.
        Amen, Amen!

Hallelujah! Hallelujah!
Praise be given
Evermore by earth and heaven. Amen.
Philip Nicolai
Tr. William Mercer

IHS

Leader: IHS is another monogram for Jesus Christ. There are several interpretations of what this monogram means but the correct explanation is that the letters IHΣ are the first three letters of the Greek word for Jesus IHΣOYΣ. When knowledge of the Greek language declined, the church substituted the Latin letter S for the Greek letter Σ *(Leader holds poster card displaying the above Greek letters.)* Joshua is the Hebrew form of Jesus. The Old Testament Joshua who was chosen to lead God's people to a new life in the Promised Land is a type of Jesus, the Savior-Shepherd, who leads his people to life eternal.

First Reader: The name Jesus means savior. It was the name given to him by God.

The angel Gabriel was sent from God unto a city of Galilee, named Nazareth, To a virgin espoused to a man whose name was Joseph, of the house of David; and the virgin's name was Mary. And the angel came in unto her, and said, Hail, thou that art highly favored, the Lord is with thee: blessed art thou among women. And when she saw him, she was troubled at his saying, and cast in her mind what manner of salutation this should be. And the angel said unto her, Fear not, Mary: for thou hast found favor with God. And, behold, thou shalt conceive in thy womb, and bring forth a son, and shalt call his name JESUS. He shall be great, and shall be called the Son of the Highest: and the Lord God shall give unto him the throne of his father David: And he shall reign over the house of Jacob for ever; and of his kingdom there shall be no end.

Second Reader: Jesus was also the name which Pilate used when our Savior was crucified.

> And Pilate wrote a title, and put it on the cross. And the writing was, JESUS OF NAZARETH THE KING OF THE JEWS. This title then read many of the Jews: for the place where Jesus was crucified was nigh to the city: and it was written in Hebrew, and Greek, and Latin. Then said the chief priests of the Jews to Pilate, Write not, The King of the Jews; but that he said, I am King of the Jews. Pilate answered, What I have written I have written.

Third Reader: The angel, sent from heaven to roll back the stone from Jesus' tomb, comforted the women who came early Sunday morning with spices to anoint his body by telling them Jesus was risen from the dead.

> In the end of the sabbath, as it began to dawn toward the first day of the week, came Mary Magdalene and the other Mary to see the sepulchre. And, behold, there was a great earthquake: for the angel of the Lord descended from heaven, and came and rolled back the stone from the door, and sat upon it . . . And the angel answered and said unto the women, Fear not ye: for I know that ye seek Jesus, which was crucified. He is not here: for he is risen, as he said. Come, see the place where the Lord lay. And go quickly, and tell his disciples that he is risen from the dead . . . And they departed quickly from the sepulchre with fear and great joy; and did run to bring his disciples word.

Leader: Let us join in singing a prayer to Jesus, our Savior, who stooped down to become a man-child, who gave his life for our sins, and who rose again so that we too can have the victory over death.

Scripture Readings: Luke 1:26–33; John 19:19–22; Matthew 28:1–2, 5–7, 8.

Song: Savior, Like a Shepherd Lead Us *(Audience)*

Savior, like a shepherd lead us,
Much we need thy tender care;
In thy pleasant pastures feed us,
For our use thy folds prepare.
Blessed Jesus, blessed Jesus,
Thou hast bought us, thine we are;
Blessed Jesus, blessed Jesus.
Thou hast bought us, thine we arc.

We are thine, do thou befriend us,
Be the guardian of our way;
Keep thy flock from sin, defend us,
Seek us when we go astray.
Blessed Jesus, blessed Jesus,
Hear thy children when they pray;
Blessed Jesus, blessed Jesus,
Hear thy children when they pray.
Dorothy A. Thrupp

Circle

Leader: A circle has no beginning and no end. That's why a circle is a very good way to show the eternity of Jesus. When three circles are linked together, they represent God the Father, Jesus the Son, and the Holy Spirit—the three persons of the Trinity. The three persons are separate, but they are also one God.

Join me in reading responsively John 14:1–21 in which Jesus explains to us the oneness of God and the different work of each Person of the Trinity.

Leader: Let not your heart be troubled: ye believe in God, believe also in me.

Audience: In my Father's house are many mansions: if it were not so, I would have told you. I go to prepare a place for you. And if I go and prepare a place for you, I will come again, and receive you unto myself; that where I am, there ye may be also. And wither I go ye know, and the way ye know.

Leader: Thomas saith unto him, Lord, we know not
whither thou goest; and how can we know the way?

Audience: Jesus saith unto him, I am the way, the truth and
the life: no man cometh unto the Father, but by me. If ye
had known me, ye should have known my Father also: and
from henceforth ye know him, and have seen him.

Leader: Philip saith unto him, Lord, shew us the Father,
and it sufficeth us.

Audience: Jesus saith unto him, Have I been so long time
with you, and yet hast thou not known me, Philip? he that
hath seen me hath seen the Father; and how sayest thou
then, Shew us the Father?

Leader: Believest thou not that I am in the Father, and the
Father in me? The words that I speak unto you I speak not
of myself: but the Father that dwelleth in me, he doeth the
works.

Audience: Believe me that I am in the Father, and the Father
in me: or else believe me for the very works' sake. Verily,
verily, I say unto you, He that believeth on me, the works
that I do shall he do also; and greater works than these
shall he do; because I go unto my Father;

Leader: And whatsoever ye shall ask in my name, that will I
do, that the Father may be glorified in the Son. If ye shall
ask any thing in my name, I will do it.

Audience: If ye love me, keep my commandments. And I
will pray the Father, and he shall give you another Com-
forter, that he may abide with you for ever; Even the Spirit
of truth; whom the world cannot receive, because it seeth
him not, neither knoweth him: but ye know him; for he
dwelleth with you, and shall be in you.

Leader: I will not leave you comfortless: I will come to you.
Yet a little while, and the world seeth me no more; but ye
see me: because I live, ye shall live also.

Audience: At that day ye shall know that I am in my Father, and ye in me, and I in you.

Leader: He that hath my commandments, and keepeth them, he it is that loveth me: and he that loveth me shall be loved of my Father, and I will love him, and will manifest myself to him.

Song: Holy! Holy! Holy! Lord God Almighty *(Audience)*

> Holy, holy, holy! Lord God Almighty!
>   Early in the morning our song shall rise to thee;
> Holy, holy, holy! merciful and mighty!
>   God in three Persons, blessed Trinity!
>
> Holy, holy, holy! all the saints adore thee,
>   Casting down their golden crowns around the glassy sea;
> Cherubim and seraphim falling down before thee,
>   Who was, and is, and evermore shalt be.
>
> Holy, holy, holy! though the darkness hide thee,
>   Though the eye of sinful man thy glory may not see;
> Only Thou are holy; there is none beside thee,
>   Perfect in power, in love, and purity.
>
> Holy, holy, holy! Lord God Almighty!
>   All thy works shall praise thy name in earth and sky and
>   sea;
> Holy, holy, holy! merciful and mighty!
>   God in three Persons, blessed Trinity!

Wheat

Leader: Since bread is made from wheat, a sheaf of wheat makes us think of Jesus' words, "I am the bread of life; he that cometh to me shall never hunger; and he that believeth on me shall never thirst" (John 6:35). When we ask him, Jesus feeds our souls with heavenly bread so that our love for him grows stronger and stronger.

Read with me from John 6:27–40 where Jesus tells us of the necessity of eating the Bread of Life.

Leader: Labor not for the meat which perisheth, but for that meat which endureth unto everlasting life, which the Son of man shall give unto you: for him hath God the Father sealed.

Audience: Then said they unto him, What shall we do, that we might work the works of God?

Leader: Jesus answered and said unto them, This is the work of God, that ye believe on him whom he hath sent.

Audience: They said therefore unto him, What sign shewest thou then, that we may see, and believe thee? What dost thou work? Our fathers did eat manna in the desert; as it is written, He gave them bread from heaven to eat.

Leader: Then Jesus said unto him, Verily, verily, I say unto you, Moses gave you not that bread from heaven; but my Father giveth you the true bread from heaven. For the bread of God is he which cometh down from heaven, and giveth life unto the world.

Audience: Then said they unto him, Lord, evermore give us this bread.

Leader: And Jesus said unto them, I am the bread of life: he that cometh to me shall never hunger; and he that believeth on me shall never thirst.

Audience: But I said unto you, That ye also have seen me, and believe not. All that the Father giveth me shall come to me; and him that cometh to me I will in no wise cast out.

Leader: For I came down from heaven, not to do mine own will, but the will of him that sent me. And this is the Father's will which hath sent me, that of all which he hath given me I should lose nothing, but should raise it up again at the last day.

Audience: And this is the will of him that sent me, that every one which seeth the Son, and believeth on him, may have everlasting life: and I will raise him up at the last day.

Song: Break Thou the Bread of Life *(Audience)*

> Break thou the bread of life, dear Lord to me,
>   As thou didst break the loaves beside the sea;
> Beyond the sacred page I seek thee, Lord;
>   My spirit pants for Thee, O living Word.
>
> Bless thou the truth, dear Lord, to me, to me,
>   As thou didst bless the bread by Galilee;
> Then shall all bondage cease, all fetters fall;
>   And I shall find my peace, my all in all.
>
> Thou art the bread of life, O Lord to me,
>   Thou holy Word the truth that saveth me,
> Give me to eat and live with thee above;
>   Teach me to love thy truth, for thou art love.
>
> O send thy Spirit, Lord, now unto me,
>   That he may touch my eyes and make me see;
> Show me the truth concealed within thy word,
>   For in thy book revealed I see thee, Lord.
>
>   William E. Sherwin

The Alpha and Omega

Alpha and Omega, the first and last symbols of the Greek alphabet, form this symbol of Christ. In Revelation 1:8 we read: "I am the Alpha and Omega, the beginning and the ending, saith the Lord God, which is, and which was, and which is to come, the Almighty."

Jesus Christ, the Word—who was the beginning (the Alpha), who created the world, who became flesh, died, and rose, who alone has the words of life—is also the Omega, the ending, the Amen, the Almighty.

Leader: John had many visions of what will happen when Jesus comes again to reign forever and ever. He saw four marvelous beasts before the throne of God who rested not day or night but continually praised Christ saying, "Holy, holy, holy, Lord God Almighty, which was, and is, and is to come."

Audience: And after these things I heard a great voice of much people in heaven, saying, Alleluia; Salvation, and glory, and honor, and power, unto the Lord our God:

Leader: And I heard as it were the voice of a great multitude, and as the voice of many waters, and as the voice of mighty thunderings, saying, Alleluia: for the Lord God omnipotent reigneth.

Audience: And I saw a new heaven and a new earth: for the first heaven and the first earth were passed away; and there was no more sea.

Leader: And I heard a great voice out of heaven saying, Behold, the tabernacle of God is with men, and he will dwell with them, and they shall be his people, and God himself shall be with them, and be their God.

Audience: And God shall wipe away all tears from their eyes; and there shall be no more death, neither sorrow, nor crying, neither shall there be any more pain: for the former things are passed away.

Leader: And he that sat upon the throne said, Behold, I make all things new. And he said unto me, Write: for these words are true and faithful.

Audience: And he said unto me, It is done. I am the Alpha and Omega, the beginning and the end. I will give unto him that is athirst of the fountain of the water of life freely. He that overcometh shall inherit all things; and I will be his God, and he shall be my Son.

Leader: And, behold, I come quickly; and my reward is with me, to give every man according as his work shall be. I am the Alpha and Omega, the beginning and the end, the first and the last.

All: He which testifieth these things saith, Surely I come quickly. Amen. Even so, come, Lord Jesus.

Scripture Readings: Revelation 4:8b; 19:1, 6; 21:1, 3–7; 22:12, 13, 20.

Song: At the Name of Jesus *(Audience)*

> At the name of Jesus
>   Every knee shall bow,
> Every tongue confess him
>   King of Glory now.
> 'Tis the Father's pleasure
>   We should call him Lord,
> Who from the beginning
>   Was the mighty Word.
>
> At his voice creation
>   Sprang at once to sight:
> All the angel faces,
>   All the hosts of light,
> Thrones and dominations,
>   Stars upon their way,
> All the heavenly orders
>   In their great array.
>
> Brothers, this Lord Jesus
>   Shall return again
> With his Father's glory,
>   With His angel-train;
> For all wreaths of empire
>   Meet upon his brow,
> And our hearts confess him
>   King of Glory now.
>   Caroline M. Noel

The Cornerstone

Leader: A cornerstone is placed at the spot where two walls of a building meet and serves to bind the walls together. When Christ is called the chief Cornerstone, that means he binds us and God together.

Sometimes a cornerstone is placed near the foundation and helps to support the rest of the building. Jesus serves as a precious Cornerstone for all who trust him for their salvation.

The Letters on the cornerstone are:

(Leader holds a poster board displaying the following list:)

IC—Jesus

XC—Christ

NIKA—Conquers

IHS—an abbreviation for Christ

First Reader: Isaiah prophesied, "Therefore thus saith the Lord God, Behold, I lay in Zion for a foundation a stone, a tried stone, a precious corner stone, a sure foundation . . ." (28:16). And the psalmist said, "I will praise thee: for thou has heard me, and art become my salvation. The stone which the builders refused is become the head stone of the corner" (118:21, 22).

Second Reader: In the Gospel of Matthew, Jesus spoke of himself as the cornerstone (21:42). Later, when Peter and John were on trial for healing a lame man in the name of Jesus, Peter spoke in their defense saying, "Be it known unto you all, and to all the people of Israel, that by the name of Jesus Christ of Nazareth, whom ye crucified, whom God raised from the dead, even by him doth this man stand here before you whole. This is the stone which was set at nought of you builders, which is become the head of the corner. Neither is there salvation in any other: for there is none other name under heaven given among men, whereby we must be saved." (Acts 4:10–12)

Third Reader: In 1 Peter 2 we are told how we ought to live if we are members of that spiritual house built on Christ the chief Cornerstone. "If so be ye have tasted that the Lord is gracious. To whom coming, as unto a living stone, disallowed indeed of men, but chosen of God, and precious, Ye also as lively stones, are built up a spiritual house, an holy priesthood, to offer up spiritual sacrifices, acceptable to God by Jesus Christ. Wherefore also it is contained in the scripture, Behold, I lay in Sion a chief corner stone, elect, precious: and he that believeth on him shall not be confounded. Unto you therefore which believe he is precious: but unto them which be disobedient, the stone which the builders disallowed, the same is made the head of the corner. And a stone of stumbling, and a rock of offence, even to them which stumble at the word, being disobedient: whereunto they were also appointed. But ye are a chosen generation, a royal priesthood, an holy nation, a peculiar people; that ye should shew forth the praises of him who hath called you out of darkness into his marvelous light." (vv. 3–9)

Song: The Church's One Foundation *(Audience)*

> The Church's one foundation
>   Is Jesus Christ, her Lord;
> She is his new creation
>   By water and the Word;
> From heaven he came and sought her
>   To be his holy bride;
> With his own blood he bought her.
>   And for her life he died.
>
> Elect from every nation,
>   Yet one o'er all the earth,
> Her charter of salvation,
>   One Lord, one faith, one birth;
> One holy name she blesses,
>   Partakes one holy food,
> And to one hope she presses,
>   With every grace endued.
>
> 'Mid toil and tribulation
>   And tumult of her war,
> She waits the consummation

Of peace forevermore;
Till with the vision glorious
Her longing eyes are blest,
And the great church victorious
Shall be the church at rest.
                    Samuel John Stone

The Sun of Righteousness

Leader: A sun with the superimposed Greek letters P and X, representing Christ, reminds us of the Messiah, the Sun of righteousness. When Malachi prophesied about the Sun of righteousness who rises with healing in his wings, he was referring to the truth that the sickness (sin) of our world is healed by the righteousness of Christ.

In many ways the sun reminds us of Jesus. It lights the earth so that we can see where we are going and find things that we couldn't see in the dark. The sun warms the earth and helps things to grow. It makes people feel healthy and happy. It is shining all the time, even when we can't see it.

Reader One: For the LORD God is a sun and shield: the LORD will give grace and glory: no good thing will he withhold from them that walk uprightly.

Audience: The Spirit of the Lord God is upon me; because the LORD hath anointed me to preach good tidings unto the meek; he hath sent me to bind up the brokenhearted, to proclaim liberty to the captives, and the opening of the prison to them that are bound.

Reader Two: To proclaim the acceptable year of the LORD, and the day of vengeance of our God; to comfort all that mourn; To appoint unto them that mourn in Zion, to give unto them beauty for ashes, the oil of joy for mourning, the garment of praise for the spirit of heaviness; that they might be called trees of righteousness, the planting of the LORD, that he might be glorified.

Audience: For Zion's sake will I not hold my peace, and for Jerusalem's sake I will not rest, until the righteousness thereof go forth as brightness, and the salvation thereof as a lamp that burneth.

Reader One: And the Gentiles shall see thy righteousness, and all kings thy glory: and thou shalt be called by a new name, which the mouth of the Lord shall name.

Audience: Thou shalt be a crown of glory in the hand of the Lord, and a royal diadem in the hand of thy God.

Reader Two: Blessed be the Lord God of Israel; for he hath visited and redeemed his people, And hath raised up an horn of salvation for us in the house of his servant David.

Audience: To give knowledge of salvation unto his people by the remission of their sins, Through the tender mercy of our God; whereby the dayspring from on high hath visited us, To give light to them that sit in darkness and in the shadow of death, to guide our feet into the way of peace.

Scripture Readings: Psalm 84:11; Isaiah 61:1–3; Isaiah 62:1–3; Luke 1:68, 69, 77–79.

Song: Beautiful Savior *(Audience)*

>   Beautiful Savior! King of creation!
>   Son of God and Son of Man!
>   Truly I'd love thee, Truly I'd serve thee,
>   Light of my soul, my joy, my crown.
>
>   Fair are the meadows, fair are the woodlands,
>   Robed in flowers of blooming spring;
>   Jesus is fairer, Jesus is purer;
>   He makes our sorrowing spirit sing.
>
>   Fair is the sunshine, fair is the moonlight,
>   Bright the sparkling stars on high;
>   Jesus shines brighter, Jesus shines purer,
>   Than all the angels in the sky.

Beautiful Savior! Lord of the nations!
Son of God and Son of Man!
Glory and honor, praise, adoration,
Now and forevermore be thine!

Crusader's Hymn

The Anchor Cross

Leader: First-century Christians carved the anchor cross on the walls of the catacombs. Non-Christians would see only an anchor but Christians would recognize the cross in the design and remember that it was Christ's death that gave them life.

In Hebrews 6:19 we are promised that all who claim God's offer of salvation have a hope (Jesus) who is a strong, firm, and secure Anchor for our lives.

First Reader: And we desire that every one of you do shew the same diligence to the full assurance of hope unto the end. . . . [That] we might have a strong consolation, who have fled for refuge to lay hold upon the hope set before us: Which hope we have as an anchor of the soul, both sure and stedfast, and which entereth into that within the veil; Whither the forerunner is for us entered, even Jesus, made an high priest for ever after the order of Melchisedec.

Second Reader: . . . for I know whom I have believed, and am persuaded that he is able to keep that which I have committed unto him against that day. Hold fast the form of sound words, which thou hast heard of me, in faith and love which is in Christ Jesus. That good thing which was committed unto thee by the Holy Ghost which dwelleth in us.

Third Reader: My little children, let us not love in word, neither in tongue; but in deed and in truth. And hereby we know that we are of the truth, and shall assure our hearts before him. For if our heart condemn us, God is greater than our heart, and knoweth all things. Beloved, if our heart condemn us not, then we have confidence toward God. And whatsoever we ask, we receive of him, because we keep his commandments, and do those things that are pleasing in his sight. And this is his commandment, that we should believe on the name of his son Jesus Christ, and love one another, as he gave us commandment. And he that keepeth his commandments dwelleth in him, and he in him. And hereby we know that he abideth in us, by the Spirit which he hath given us.

Scripture Readings: Hebrews 6:11, 18b–20; 2 Timothy 1:12–14; 1 John 3:18–24.

Song: I Know Not Why God's Wondrous Grace *(Audience)*

> I know not why God's wondrous grace
>   To me he has made known,
> Nor why, unworthy, Christ in love
>   Redeemed me for his own.
>
> Refrain:
> But I know whom I have believed,
>   And am persuaded that he is able
> To keep that which I've committed
>   Unto him against that day.
>
> I know not how this saving faith
>   To me he did impart,
> Nor how believing in his Word
>   Brought peace within my heart.
>
> I know not how the Spirit moves,
>   Convincing men of sin,
> Revealing Jesus through the Word,
>   Creating faith in him.
>
> I know not what of good or ill
>   May be reserved for me,
> Of weary ways or golden days,
>   Before his face I see.
>   Daniel W. Whittle

Advent Rose

Leader: An advent symbol from the thirteenth century, the
rose is a good reminder of Christ's birth because it is a
lovely, fragrant flower that bursts out of what seems like a
dead-looking twig. Christ came as a beautiful love-gift
from God when most people gave up all hope of ever seeing
the promised Messiah. When Christ lives in our hearts,
our lives will blossom with joy and happiness.

Several times Isaiah, in his prophecy, speaks of the desert blossoming like a rose at Jesus' coming. Let us read
responsively from these beautiful words of the prophet.

The wilderness and the solitary place shall be glad for
them; and the desert shall rejoice, and blossom as the
rose.

Audience: It shall blossom abundantly, and rejoice even
with joy and singing: the glory of Lebanon shall be given
unto it, the excellency of Carmel and Sharon, they shall
see the glory of the LORD, and the excellency of our God.

Leader: Strengthen ye the weak hands, and confirm the
feeble knees. Say to them that are of a fearful heart, Be
strong, fear not; behold, your God will come with vengeance, even God with a recompence; he will come and
save you.

Audience: Then the eyes of the blind shall be opened, and
the ears of the deaf shall be unstopped. Then shall the lame
man leap as an hart, and the tongue of the dumb sing: for in
the wilderness shall waters break out, and streams in the
desert.

Leader: For the Lord shall comfort Zion: he will comfort
all her waste places; and he will make her wilderness like
Eden, and her desert like the garden of the LORD; joy and
gladness shall be found therein, thanksgiving, and the
voice of melody.

Audience: For ye shall go out with joy, and be led forth with peace: the mountains and the hills shall break forth before you into singing, and all the trees of the field clap their hands.

Leader: Instead of the thorn shall come up the fir tree, and instead of the brier shall come up the myrtle tree: and it shall be to the LORD for a name, for an everlasting sign that shall not be cut off.

Scripture Readings: Isaiah 35:1–6; 51:3; 55:12, 13

Song: Lo, How a Rose E'er Blooming *(Audience)*

> Lo, how a rose e'er blooming
> From tender stem hath sprung!
> O Jesse's lineage coming
> As men of old have sung.
>> It came, a flow'ret bright,
>> Amid the cold of winter,
>> When half spent was the night.
>
> Isaiah 'twas foretold it.
> The Rose I have in mind,
> With Mary we behold it,
> The Virgin mother kind.
>> To show God's love aright
>> She bore to men a Savior,
>> When half spent was the night.
>>> 15th Century German
>>> Tr. Theodore Baker

3

Advent
Past, Present, and Future

Prelude: "O Come, O Come, Emmanuel"

Advent: A Celebration of the Past

Scene I

Narrator: The season of Advent is a celebration of the past, present, and future. The birth of Jesus Christ is a celebration of Advent past. Going back in time, almost two thousand years ago, we enter the town of Nazareth. It is a Sabbath day before the birth of Christ. Mary and her friend Salome are returning from a worship service in the synagogue.

Mary: Oh, how I wish the Messiah would come soon!

Salome: Do you think we will see him when he comes?

Mary: I don't know. The prophets say he will be born in Bethlehem, but he will be king in Nazareth too.

Salome: Yes, I remember hearing something about the province of Galilee at the synagogue this morning.

Mary: "He will grieviously afflict her by the way of the sea, beyond Jordan, in Galilee of the nations. The people that walked in darkness have seen a great light; they that dwell in the land of the shadow of death, upon them hath the light shined."

Salome: "For unto us a child is born, unto us a son is given: and the government shall be upon his shoulder: and his name shall be called Wonderful, Counselor, the mighty God, the everlasting Father, the Prince of Peace."

Mary and Salome: "Of the increase of his government and peace there shall be no end, upon the throne of David, and upon his kingdom, to order it, and to establish it with judgment and with justice from henceforth even for ever."

Mary: What a great King he will be!

Scripture Readings: Isaiah 9:2; 6–7.

Scene II

Narrator: Later that day, Mary is alone. Gabriel, a messenger from God, enters her room.

Gabriel: Greetings, the Lord is with you. *(Mary shrinks back.)* Don't be afraid, Mary, the Lord is pleased with you. You are going to have a son. He will be the great Messiah for whom you have been praying.

Mary: But how can that be? I don't have a husband yet.

Gabriel: Your child will be the Son of God, Emmanuel. With God, nothing is impossible.

Scene III

Narrator: It was a long walk from Galilee to the hill country of Judea but Mary needed this time alone to prepare for the miracle which would happen to her. God knew she would need someone with whom to share her wonderful news. Gabriel told her that Elizabeth, her elderly cousin, who had given up all hope of having a child, was going to have a baby son. She was just the person Mary must see.

Mary had many unanswered questions: How can I make Joseph understand that I have not been unfaithful to him? If Joseph refuses to take me as his wife, how can I take care of this child properly? How is it possible that the

Messiah will be born in Bethlehem when my home is in Nazareth?

With Gabriel's last words echoing through her mind, "With God nothing is impossible," Mary arrived at the home of Zechariah and Elizabeth. She didn't even have to explain her visit to her cousin. As soon as Mary greeted her, Elizabeth knew that she was to be the mother of the Savior.

Elizabeth: Mary! when you spoke to me just now, the baby inside of me jumped for joy. You are the most honored of all women. And to think that you have come to visit me!

Mary: Praise the Lord! I rejoice in God my Savior. He has remembered the promises he gave to Abraham generations ago. And he has chosen me, a poor village girl, to be the mother of His Son.

Narrator: Mary stayed with Elizabeth for three months. In time God answered each of the questions which had troubled her. He kept all of his promises to the minutest detail. "With God nothing is impossible." God even controlled the affairs of the great Roman Empire, so that Jesus would be born in Bethlehem.

Songs: O Little Town of Bethlehem *(Audience)*

>   O little town of Bethlehem,
>   How still we see thee lie!
>   Above thy deep and dreamless sleep
>   The silent stars go by:
>   Yet in thy dark streets shineth
>   The everlasting Light;
>   The hopes and fears of all the years
>   Are met in thee tonight.
>
>   For Christ is born of Mary;
>   And gathered all above,
>   While mortals sleep, the angels keep
>   Their watch of wondering love.

O morning stars, together
Proclaim the holy birth,
And praises sing to God the King
And peace to men on earth.
Phillips Brooks

Joy to the World

Joy to the world! The Lord is come;
Let earth receive her King;
Let every heart prepare him room,
And heaven and nature sing.

Joy to the earth! The Savior reigns;
Let men their songs employ;
While fields and floods, rocks, hills,
   and plains
Repeat the sounding joy.
Isaac Watts

Advent: A Celebration for the Present

(A Christmas tree is center stage with a group of children gathered around. The gifts which the children hold are symbols of God's gifts to us. The children could make their own gifts in Sunday school classes before Advent. They may have ideas for gifts which are not mentioned in the skit.)

Narrator: In the celebration of the Advent present, we as Christians must remember the significance Advent has for today. For God so loved the world, that he gave his only begotten Son, that whosoever believeth in him should not perish, but have everlasting life (John 3:16).

God not only gave his Son, Jesus Christ, but he also gave his people many other gifts. In his letter to the Ephesians Paul writes, But unto every one of us is given grace according to the measure of the gift of Christ. . . . When he ascended up on high, he led captivity captive, and gave gifts unto men (Eph. 4:7, 8).

We return his gifts in giving to others. The tree itself is a symbol of everlasting life and we will adorn it with the gifts God has given to us.

Love: We love him, because he first loved us (1 John 4:19).

Word: Let the word of Christ dwell in you richly in all wisdom . . . singing with grace in your hearts to the Lord (Col. 3:16).

Faith: For by grace are ye saved through faith; and that not of yourselves: it is the gift of God (Eph. 2:8).

Life: I am come that they might have life, and that they might have it more abundantly (John 10:10).

Peace: Be careful for nothing; but in every thing by prayer and supplication with thanksgiving let your requests be made known unto God. And the peace of God, which passeth all understanding, shall keep your hearts and minds through Christ Jesus (Phil. 4:6, 7).

Truth: Jesus said, ". . . I am the way, the truth, and the life: no man cometh unto the Father, but by me" (John 14:6).

Light: Jesus said, ". . . I am the light of the world: he that followeth me shall not walk in darkness, but shall have the light of life" (John 8:12).

Power: But ye shall receive power, after that the Holy Ghost is come upon you: and ye shall be witnesses unto me both in Jerusalem, and in all Judea, and in Samaria, and unto the uttermost part of the earth (Acts 1:8).

Forgiveness: Be it known unto you . . . that through this man [Jesus] is preached unto you the forgiveness of sins (Acts 13:38).

Joy: These things have I spoken unto you, that my joy might remain in you, and that your joy might be full (John 15:11).

Wisdom: If any of you lack wisdom, let him ask of God, that giveth to all men liberally . . . and it shall be given him (James 1:5).

Patience: But if we hope for that we see not, then do we with patience wait for it (Rom. 8:25).

Hope: To whom God would make known what is the riches of the glory of this mystery among the Gentiles; which is Christ in you, the hope of glory (Col. 1:27).

Narrator: May these gifts of God fill your hearts and lives in this Christmas season, and throughout the days to come until Jesus' future advent.

Songs: Now God Be Praised *(Audience)*

Now God be praised in heaven above,
   Praised be he for his great love,
Wherein all creatures live and move,
   Alleluia! Alleluia! Alleluia!

Praise him yet more for conquering faith,
   Which feareth neither pain nor death,
But trusting God, rejoicing saith,
   Alleluia! Alleluia! Alleluia!

His grace defends us from all ill;
   His Christ shall be our leader still,
Till heaven and earth shall do his will;
   Alleluia! Alleluia! Alleluia!

                    Author unknown

Praise, My Soul, the King of Heaven

Praise, my soul, the King of heaven,
   To his feet your tribute bring;
Ransomed, healed, restored, forgiven,
   Who, like me, his praise should sing.
Alleluia! Alleluia! Praise the everlasting King!

Fatherlike, he tends and spares us;
   Well our feeble frame he knows,
In his hands he gently bears us,
   Rescues us from all our foes.
Alleluia! Alleluia! Widely as his mercy flows!

Angels, help us to adore him,
    You behold him face to face;
Sun and moon, bow down before him;
    Dwellers in all time and space.
Alleluia! Alleluia! Praise with us the God of grace!
                                        Henry Francis Lyte

Advent: A Celebration for the Future

Narrator: For the child of God Christmas is not merely a celebration of past events. It is also an expression of the hope for Christ's advent at the end of time. The foreseeing of the Messiah's first coming by Old Testament prophets and the details of Christ's return provided by John in the Book of Revelation merge in the significance of God in our lives.

Jesus' second coming will be climaxed with the wedding feast of Christ and his Bride. It will be that perfect marriage in which all who belong to him will find their ultimate freedom and fulfillment.

The following selections from Revelation and Isaiah illustrate how Christ's life is intertwined with ours. Let us participate in these readings with joy.

And after these things I heard a great voice of much people in heaven, saying,

All: Alleluia; Salvation, and glory, and honor, and power, unto the Lord our God: For true and righteous are his judgments.

Narrator: And the four and twenty elders and the four beasts fell down and worshiped God that sat on the throne, saying,

All: Amen; Alleluia!

Narrator: And a voice came out of the throne, saying,

All: Praise our God, all ye his servants, and ye that fear him, both small and great.

Narrator: And I heard as it were the voice of a great multitude, and as the voice of many waters, and as the voice of mighty thunderings, saying,

All: Alleluia: for the Lord God omnipotent reigneth.
Let us be glad and rejoice, and give honor to him:
for the marriage of the Lamb is come,
and his wife hath made herself ready.
And to her was granted that she should be arrayed
in fine linen, clean and white: for the fine linen
is the righteousness of saints. . . .
Blessed are they which are called unto the marriage
supper of the Lamb.

Narrator: And I saw a new heaven and a new earth: for the first heaven and the first earth were passed away; and there was no more sea. And I . . . saw the holy city, new Jerusalem, coming down from God out of heaven, prepared as a bride adorned for her husband. And I heard a great voice out of heaven saying,

Reader One: Behold, the tabernacle of God is with men,
and he will dwell with them,
and they shall be his people,
and God himself shall be with them, and be their God.
And God shall wipe away all tears from their eyes;
and there shall be no more death,
neither sorrow, nor crying,
neither shall there be any more pain:
for the former things are passed away.

Narrator: And he that sat up on the throne said,

Reader Two: Behold, I make all things new . . .
It is done!
I am Alpha and Omega, the beginning and the end.
I will give unto him that is athirst of the
fountain of the water of life freely.

Narrator: And there came unto me one of the seven angels
. . . saying,

Reader Three: Come hither, I will shew thee the bride, the Lamb's wife.

Narrator: And he carried me away in the spirit to a great and high mountain, and shewed me that great city, the holy Jerusalem, descending out of heaven from God, having the glory of God: and her light was like unto a stone most precious, even as a jasper stone, clear as crystal.

Reader Four: And, behold, I come quickly; and my reward is with me, to give to every man according as his work shall be. I am the Alpha and Omega, the beginning and the end, the first and the last. Blessed are they that do his commandments, that they may have right to the tree of life, and may enter in through the gates into the city.

All: I will greatly rejoice in the LORD,
    my soul shall be joyful in my God;
for he hath clothed me with the garments of salvation,
he hath covered me with the robe of righteousness,
as a bridegroom decketh himself with ornaments,
and as a bride adorneth herself with her jewels.

Narrator: The Spirit and the bride say,

All: Come! And let him that heareth say, Come!
And let him that is athirst come.
And whosoever will, let him take the water of life
    freely.

Narrator: He which testifieth these things saith,
    "Surely I come quickly."

All: Amen! Even so, come Lord Jesus!

Scripture Readings: Revelation 19:1–2, 4–9; 21:1–6, 9–11; 22:12–14, 17, 20; Isaiah 61:10.

Song: All Hail the Power of Jesus' Name *(Audience)*

All hail the power of Jesus' name!
Let angels prostrate fall;

Bring forth the royal diadem,
  And crown him Lord of all!

O that with yonder sacred throng
  We at his feet may fall!
We'll join the everlasting song,
  And crown him Lord of all!
             Edward Perronet

(*An appropriate postlude would be the Hallelujah Chorus from Handel's* Messiah.)

4

The Majestic Lord

The following program is designed to show the majesty of our Lord at creation, at Sinai, in Isaiah's prophecy, in his resurrection and in his return as King of kings. It would be appropriate to perform as an Advent or Easter pageant or as a church school celebration exalting the Word of God.

Creation

(The voice choir appears center stage with the instrumentalists just off stage. A drum roll could be used instead of the French horn or various piano chords could be played in lieu of the other instruments.)

Low Voice: Let all the earth fear the LORD: let all the inhabitants of the world stand in awe of him. For he spake, and it was done; he commanded, and it stood fast. *(cymbal)*

All: In the beginning was the Word, and the Word was with God, and the Word was God.

Medium Voice: All things were made by him: and without him was not anything made that was made. *(cymbal)*

High Voice: And the earth was without form, and void;

All: And darkness was upon the face of the deep.

Low Voice: And the Spirit of God moved upon the face of the waters. *(triangle)*

All: The heavens declare the glory of God; *(french horn)* and the firmament sheweth his handywork. *(cymbal)*

Medium Voice: The earth is the LORD's, and the fulness thereof; the world, and they that dwell therein.

Low Voice: For he hath founded it upon the sea, and established it upon the floods.

All: O LORD, how manifold are thy works! *(cymbal)* In wisdom hast thou made them all: the earth is full of thy riches. *(french horn)*

High Voice: The glory of the LORD shall endure forever: the LORD shall rejoice in his works. *(cymbal)*

All: *(with heads bowed)* The eyes of all wait upon thee; and thou givest them their meat in due season. *(triangle)* Thou openest thine hand, and satisfiest the desire of every living thing. *(triangle)*

Low Voice: Make a joyful noise unto the LORD, all ye lands.

Medium Voice: O give thanks unto the LORD; call upon his name:

High Voice: Make known his deeds among the people.

All: Sing unto him, sing psalms unto him: talk ye of all his wondrous works. He is the LORD our God: his judgments are in all the earth. *(french horn and cymbal)*

Scripture Readings: Psalm 33:8, 9; John 1:1, 3; Genesis 1:2; Psalm 19:1; Psalm 24:1, 2; Psalm 104:24, 31; Psalm 145:15, 16; Psalm 100:1; Psalm 105:1, 2, 7.

Song: Let All Mortal Flesh Keep Silence *(Audience)*

> Let all mortal flesh keep silence,
>   And with fear and trembling stand;
> Ponder nothing earthly-minded,
>   For with blessing in his hand,

Christ our God to earth descendeth,
  Our full homage to demand.

King of kings, yet born of Mary,
  As of old on earth he stood,
Lord of lords, in human vesture,
  In the body and the blood,
He will give to all the faithful
  His own self for heavenly food.

Rank on rank the host of heaven
  Spreads its vanguard on the way,
As the Light of light descendeth
  From the realms of endless day,
That the powers of hell may vanish
  As the darkness clears away.

At his feet the six-winged seraph;
  Cherubim, with sleepless eye,
Veil their faces to the presence,
  As with ceaseless voice they cry,
"Alleluia, Alleluia, Alleluia, Lord Most High!"
                           Liturgy of St. James
                           Tr. Gerard Moultrie

The Law

(The reading of the Law may be done entirely by a voice choir or by a narrator and group speaking responsively. A pantomime choir should be center stage dressed in simple costumes appropriate to the time of Moses and the Israelites at Sinai. The presentation would be quite effective if the readers spoke from off-stage or from a balcony. Be sure the words can be clearly understood by the audience.)

Narration: And Moses brought forth the people out of the camp to meet with God; and they stood at the nether part of the mount. And mount Sinai

Pantomime Choir representing the Israelites with faces averted, and expressions of fear.

was altogether on a smoke, because the LORD descended upon it in fire . . . And when the voice of the trumpet sounded long, and waxed louder and louder, Moses spake, and God answered him by a voice.

And God spake all these words, saying, I am the Lord thy God, which have brought thee out of the land of Egypt, out of the house of bondage. Thou shalt have no other gods before me.

Turn toward voices, kneel in awe with heads bowed.

Thou shalt not make unto thee any graven images, or any likeness of any thing that is in heaven above, or that is in the earth beneath, or that is in the water under the earth:

Rise, making sweeping gestures upward, then sweeping gestures downward.

Thou shalt not bow down thyself to them, nor serve them: for I the LORD thy God am a jealous God, visiting the iniquity of the fathers upon the children unto the third and fourth generation of them that hate me;

Divide into two groups, and stand back to back.

And shewing mercy unto thousands of them that love me, and keep my commandments.

The two groups turn and face each other.

Thou shalt not take the name of the LORD thy God in

Stand with hands on mouths, followed

vain; for the LORD will not hold him guiltless that taketh his name in vain.

Remember the sabbath day, to keep it holy. Six days shalt thou labour, and do all thy work: But the seventh day is the sabbath of the LORD thy God: in it thou shalt not do any work, thou, nor thy son, nor thy daughter, thy manservant, nor thy maidservant, nor thy cattle, nor thy stranger that is within thy gates: For in six days the LORD made heaven and earth, the sea, and all that in them is, and rested the seventh day: wherefore the Lord blessed the sabbath day, and hallowed it.

Honor thy father and thy mother: that thy days may be long upon the land which the LORD thy God giveth thee.

Thou shalt not kill.

Thou shalt not commit adultery.

Thou shalt not steal.

by hands raised to heaven.

Kneel with heads bowed in an attitude of worship.

Slowly rise. Group divides in half; each half faces the other with arms outstretched.

Groups continue to face each other, but with clenched fists and tense angry faces.

Turn eyes heavenward with arms crossed on chest.

Groups crouch, shade eyes, turn back to

Thou shalt not bear false
witness against thy neighbor.

Thou shalt not covet thy
neighbour's house, thou shalt
not covet thy neighbor's wife,
nor his manservant, nor his
maidservant, nor his ox, nor
his ass, nor any thing that is
thy neighbor's.

And all the people saw the
thunderings, and the light-
nings, and the noise of the
trumpet, and the mountain
smoking: and when the people
saw it, they removed, and
stood afar off.

back, and walk
away from one an-
other.

Form pairs, left hands
on hips, right in
handshake.

Group forms a circle,
arms around one
another's waists.
Move in a circle,
first clockwise four
steps then back to
original positions.

Group hastily sepa-
rates, moves back
to averted faces and
expressions of fear.

Scripture Reading: Exodus 19:17–19; 20:1–18.

Song: Immortal, Invisible, God Only Wise *(Audience)*

Immortal, invisible, God only wise,
In light inaccessible hid from our eyes,
Most blessed, most glorious, the Ancient of Days,
Almighty, victorious, thy great name we praise.

To all, life thou givest to both great and small;
In all life thou livest, the true life of all;
We blossom and flourish as leaves on the tree,
And wither and perish, but naught changeth
thee.

Great Father of glory, pure Father of light,
Thine angels adore thee, all veiling their sight;

All praise we would render; O help us to see
'Tis only the splendor of light hideth thee.
Walter C. Smith

The Prophecies

(The voice chorus is center-back stage, narrator is left stage, and Isaiah is kneeling center stage, gazing upward. There is a writing table, a chair and a scroll at front-right stage.)

Narrator: No one could keep the commandments, but God promised a savior who would not only keep the Law perfectly, but who would also die for the sins of his people. Some of the richest promises of that savior were given through the prophet Isaiah.

In the year that King Uzziah died Isaiah had a vision of the Lord sitting on a throne, high and lifted up. Above him stood seraphim praising God and saying: "Holy, holy, holy, is the LORD of hosts: the whole earth is full of his glory."

Isaiah: *(looking down)* "Woe is me! for I am undone; because I am a man of unclean lips, and I dwell in the midst of a people of unclean lips: for mine eyes have seen the King, the LORD of hosts."

Narrator: Then one of the seraphim flew to him, having in his hand a burning coal which he had taken with tongs from the altar. He touched Isaiah's mouth and said, "Lo, this hath touched thy lips; and thine iniquity is taken away, and thy sin purged." Then the voice of the Lord spoke, "Whom shall I send, and who will go for us?"

Isaiah: *(arms outstretched)* "Here am I; send me."

Narrator: God said, "Go and tell this people. . . ."

(Isaiah rises slowly, crosses to the table, seats himself, opens the scroll and begins to write.)

Voice Chorus: Behold, a virgin shall conceive, and bear a son, and shall call his name Immanuel.

Isaiah: For unto us a child is born, unto us a son is given;

Voice Chorus: And the government shall be upon his shoulder: and his name shall be called Wonderful, Counselor, The mighty God, The everlasting Father, The Prince of Peace.

Isaiah: He is despised and rejected of men;

Voice Chorus: A man of sorrows, and acquainted with grief.

Isaiah: Surely he hath borne our griefs,

Voice Chorus: And carried our sorrows.

Isaiah: But he was wounded for our transgressions, he was bruised for our iniquities:

Voice Chorus: The chastisement of our peace was upon him; and with his stripes we are healed.

Isaiah: All we like sheep have gone astray; we have turned everyone to his own way;

Voice Chorus: And the LORD hath laid on him the iniquity of us all.

Isaiah: And he made his grave with the wicked, and with the rich in his death.

Voice Chorus: And the glory of the LORD shall be revealed, and all flesh shall see it together: for the mouth of the LORD hath spoken it.

Isaiah: The grass withereth, the flower fadeth . . . surely the people is grass.

Voice Chorus: But the word of our God shall stand for ever.

Scripture Readings: Isaiah 6:1–3, 5–9; 7:14; 9:6; 53:3–6, 9; 40:5, 7, 8.

Song: How Firm a Foundation *(Audience)*

> How firm a foundation, ye saints of the Lord,
>   Is laid for your faith in his excellent Word!
> What more can he say than to you he hath said,
>   To you who for refuge to Jesus have fled?
>
> "Fear not, I am with thee, O be not dismayed;
>   I am thy God, and will still give thee aid;
> I'll strengthen thee, help thee, and cause thee to stand,
>   Upheld by my righteous, omnipotent hand.
>
> "The soul that on Jesus hath leaned for repose,
>   I will not, I will not desert to his foes;
> That soul, though all hell should endeavor to shake,
>   I'll never, no, never, no, never forsake."
> > "K" in Rippon's
> > Selection of Hymns

The Word Fulfilled

Narrator: There is therefore now no condemnation to them which are in Christ Jesus . . . for what the law could not do . . . God sending his own Son in the likeness of sinful flesh, and for sin, condemned sin in the flesh: That the righteousness of the law might be fulfilled in us. . . . (Rom. 8:1, 3, 4)

Voice Chorus: In the beginning was the Word, and the Word was with God, and the Word was God. (John 1:1)

Solo Voice: And the Word was made flesh, and dwelt among us, (and we beheld his glory, the glory as of the only begotten of the Father,) full of grace and truth. (John 1:14)

Voice Chorus: . . . Christ died for our sins according to the scriptures . . . he was buried, and . . . rose again the third day . . .

Solo Voice: But now is Christ risen from the dead, and become the firstfruits of them that slept.

Voice Chorus: For since by man came death, by man came also the resurrection of the dead. (1 Cor. 15:3, 4, 20, 21)

Solo Voice: For as in Adam all die, even so in Christ shall all be made alive. But every man in his own order: Christ the firstfruits; afterward they that are Christ's at his coming. (1 Cor. 15:22, 23)

Songs: Hark! the Herald Angels Sing *(Audience)*

> Hark! the herald angels sing,
>   "Glory to the newborn King;
> Peace on earth, and mercy mild,
>   God and sinners reconciled!"
> Joyful, all ye nations, rise,
>   Join the triumph of the skies;
> With the angelic host proclaim,
>   "Christ is born in Bethlehem."
>
> Refrain:
>   Hark! the herald angels sing,
>   "Glory to the newborn King!"
>
> Christ, by highest heaven adored;
>   Christ, the everlasting Lord!
> Late in time behold him come,
>   Offspring of the virgin's womb.
> Veiled in flesh the Godhead see;
>   Hail the incarnate deity,
> Pleased as man with men to dwell,
>   Jesus, our Emmanuel.
>
> Hail the heavenborn Prince of peace!
>   Hail the Sun of righteousness!
> Light and life to all he brings,
>   Risen with healing in his wings,
> Mild he lays his glory by,
>   Born that man no more may die,
> Born to raise the sons of earth,
>   Born to give them second birth.
>   Charles Wesley

Lo, He Comes, with Clouds Descending

Lo! he comes, with clouds descending,
    Once for favored sinners slain!
Thousand, thousand saints attending
    Swell the triumph of his train;
Alleluia! Alleluia!
    God appears on earth to reign.

Every eye shall now behold him
    Robed in dreadful majesty;
Those who set at naught and sold him
    Pierced and nailed him to the tree,
Deeply wailing, deeply wailing,
    Shall the true Messiah see.

Yea, Amen! let all adore thee,
    High on thine eternal throne!
Savior, take the power and glory;
    Claim the kingdom for thine own.
O come quickly, O come quickly!
    Everlasting God, come down.
                                            Charles Wesley

Narrator: When the apostle John was in exile on the island of Patmos, he was given a vision of the glorified Christ and a revelation of future events. He heard a loud voice like a trumpet saying, "Write the things which thou hast seen, and the things which are, and the things which shall be hereafter." (Rev. 1:19)

Voice Chorus: Blessed is he that readeth, and they that hear the words of this prophecy, and keep those things which are written therein: for the time is at hand. (Rev. 1:3)

Solo Voice: I am the Alpha and Omega, the beginning and the ending, saith the Lord, which is, and which was, and which is to come, the Almighty. (Rev. 1:8)

Voice Chorus: Behold he cometh with clouds; and every eye shall see him, and they also which pierced him: and all kindreds of the earth shall wail because of him. (Rev. 1:7)

Solo Voice: These sayings are faithful and true: and the Lord God of the holy prophets sent his angels to shew unto his servants the things which must shortly be done. (Rev. 22:6)

Voice Chorus: Behold, I come quickly: blessed is he that keepeth the sayings of the prophecy of this book. (Rev. 22:7)

All: Even so, come. Lord Jesus. (Rev. 22:20)

Songs: All Hail the Power of Jesus' Name *(Audience)*

All hail the power of Jesus' name!
  Let angels prostrate fall;
Bring forth the royal diadem,
  And crown him Lord of all.

Let every kindred, every tribe,
  On this terrestrial ball,
To him all majesty ascribe,
  And crown him Lord of all.

O that with yonder sacred throng,
  We at his feet may fall;
We'll join the everlasting song,
  And crown him Lord of all.
Edward Perronet

Crown Him with Many Crowns

Crown him with many crowns,
  The Lamb upon his throne;
Hark! how the heavenly anthem drowns
  All music but its own;
Awake, my soul, and sing
  Of him who died for thee,
And hail him as thy matchless King
  Through all eternity.

Crown him the Lord of years,
  The potentate of time,

Creator of the rolling spheres,
   Ineffably sublime.
All hail, Redeemer, hail!
   For thou hast died for me;
Thy praise shall never, never fail
   Throughout eternity.

                              Matthew Bridges

Christmas Programs

5

The New Toy that Didn't Know About Christmas

Characters

Part One: 12 toys, one announcer

Part Two: 16 parts, one announcer

Note: The second part could be done by itself as a short skit. Just leave out the first lines of the announcer introducing the scene and leave out the last two sentences of the announcer's final lines as well as the lines of the toys at the end.

Part One

Costumes for each toy

Clock—Make a five- or six-foot cardboard cutout of a grandfather clock.

Game—Put a strap on a board game (e.g., SORRY) and hang it from the child's neck. You could make an appropriate hat to match the game.

Jack-in-the-Box—Use a large decorated carton from which the youngster can pop up to do his parts. He should wear a stocking cap.

Wind-up Toy—Have the child dress like a clown and attach a large cardboard key to his back.

New Toy—Any strange outer-space-type costume will do.

Innkeeper—Needs a coat, hat, gloves, and scarf.

Cast

Announcer	Game	Music Box
Raggedy Ann	Fashion Doll	Wooden Soldier
Teddy Bear	Ballerina	Wind-up Toy
Clock	Jack-in-the-Box	Shopkeeper

(The scene opens with all the toys standing stiff and still. They will not move until the shopkeeper leaves.)

Clock: Tick-tock, tick-tock. *(continue softly as Announcer and Shopkeeper speak)*

Announcer: The scene opens at closing time in a toy shop just a few days before Christmas. The shopkeeper has just finished counting the receipts from the day and is about to lock up his store for the night.

Shopkeeper: Only a few more days until Christmas! It sure would be nice to sell all these lovely toys. They would make many a boy and girl very happy. Maybe it will make the toys happy too. *(puts on hat, scarf, and coat)* The toys are sure lucky they don't have to go out on a snowy night like this. Br-r-r. *(looks around at the toys)* I just wonder what you all do while I'm gone. When I was young I used to imagine you all came to life when no one was around. What a crazy thought! *(shakes head and leaves)*

Clock: Tick-tock, tick-tock *(pauses, then speaks in this tick-tock way)* I think - the store - keeper - has gone.

Woody: Yes, I can hear him going down the sidewalk.

Music Box: That was close! For a minute I thought maybe the shopkeeper really knew what we do when he leaves at night.

Teddy Bear: Only a few more days 'til Christmas. *(hugs himself in excitement)*

New Toy: Christmas?

Doll: I can hardly wait. I'm so excited to see my new owner.

Jack: *(pops up)* Oh, oh, will Christmas ever come?

New Toy: Christmas?

Raggedy Ann: *(flops as she speaks)* How much longer? The last few days before Christmas will never go by!

New Toy: Christmas?

Ballerina: *(dancing around)* I just can't sit still; the suspense is driving me crazy.

Music Box: Have you ever stopped to think what it would be like if no one bought you?

Woody: That's just too horrible to think about.

Ballerina: You two don't worry so; someone will buy us. You know there is always that last-minute rush of shopping.

Bear: That's right: lots and lots of hustle and bustle.

Jack: *(pops up)* If no one buys me I'll hide down inside my box and never come up again.

Wind-up Toy: I doubt that, but it sure would be nice starting right now!

Game: Hey, let's not fight and worry. How about playing a game to pass the time? Oops, can't do that—toys can't play games.

Clock: Time goes - by slow - when you - have to - wait.

Music Box: Yes, it does and you certainly should know: we hear your tick-tock all night and day.

Jack: *(pops up)* Hey, I just popped up with a good idea. How about "show and tell"? We show ourselves and tell whatever we want. That could take up a lot of the time 'til Christmas.

New Toy: Christmas?

Ballerina: That sounds like a pretty good idea. I'll go first.

Wind-up Toy: No way! I'll go first.

Clock: Why fight - about - it we - will all - get a - turn.

Game: Let me organize this. You know games are always good for organizing. *(pause)* We will start at this end. You go first Teddy.

(Each toy comes to center stage for its turn)

Bear: Okay. I'm a bear who likes honey and candy. I don't care about money and I don't care if a boy or girl gets me for Christmas as long as they hug me. *(hugs himself)*

New Toy: Christmas?

Raggedy Ann: I don't care who gets me either, but I sure hope that they have Raggedy Andy.

Woody: I'm a soldier like the ones that guard Buckingham Palace. I hope my new owner has something for me to guard and that he keeps me all shined up.

Ballerina: *(twirls around)* I can't imagine a boy wanting me, so I hope a cute little girl who likes to dance as much as I do gets me. *(twirls again)*

Doll: Oh, goody! My turn! I can do many things. See? I can open and shut my eyes. I can drink from a cup and I have my very own suitcase of clothes. Inside I have slacks, shoes, blouses, and even a Christmas party dress.

New Toy: Christmas?

Wind-up Toy: Cut out the chatter, doll. It's my turn. Look, just wind me up to make me work. *(does a few turns)* See, I can spin around any time, any place, and for any body.

Doll: So that explains why you are so mean. You're just traveling in circles all the time.

Jack: I'm called a Jack-in-the-Box. All you do is push the button on my side and I pop up like this. *(pops up)* Boys and girls like me. Parents like me better because I don't need batteries.

Music Box: I don't take batteries either and I make lovely music all the time. One only needs to wind my key. So I'm very nice to have around.

Clock: I am - an ed - u ca - tion al - toy for - all girls - and boys. I teach - how to - tell time.

Game: We all do what we were made for, and I'm sure everyone is very good at what they do. But I'm a toy that more than one youngster can use at a time. I'm a game and I am great at any time of the year; especially on a rainy or stormy afternoon.

Music Box: Now that "show and tell" is done, what do we do next?

Raggedy Ann: Wait a minute. We didn't hear from the New Toy. He has been very quiet except for saying "Christmas" all the time.

New Toy: Christmas?

Raggedy Ann: You are new this year. What is your name?

New Toy: Name?

Raggedy Ann: Yes, name. *(points to herself)* My name is Ann. *(points to the others)* Each one of us has a name.

Music Box: Here, I'll tell you everyone's name. This is

Teddy, Woody, Dancer, Barbie, Windy, Jack, Tick-tock, and Game. *(each toy acknowledges his or her name in turn)* My name is Merrily.

New Toy: Name, O.S.

Raggedy Ann: That's a strange name! It doesn't seem to mean anything. Where do you come from?

New Toy: *(pointing up)* Go home!

Wind-up Toy: Go home? Up there? That's impossible! Is he crazy or something?

Music Box: Shush, Windy, that's no way to treat a guest.

New Toy: O.S, go home!

Game: I'll bet the O.S. stands for Outer Space.

Doll: Every year there seems to be a new toy on the market. I'm glad dolls are always so popular.

Bear: Bears, too. We are so cuddly! *(hugs himself)*

Ballerina: What about the Wookie from a few years ago? He certainly was cuddly.

Woody: Then a couple of years ago it was that strange little green guy; Yoda was his name, I think. And then the next year there was a toy called E.T.

Doll: And now it looks as if we have another strange green creature.

Wind-up Toy: They seem to get stranger every year! What is this world coming to?

Raggedy Ann: Don't listen to them O.S. They are just jealous that they're not as popular as you are.

Doll: Now that we have introduced each other, what else can we do to pass the time until Christmas?

New Toy: Christmas?

Wind-up Toy: Does he have to say "Christmas" every time the word is mentioned?

Game: Wouldn't you? He really doesn't know what Christmas is all about. In fact, from the way some of you are behaving, I think you don't know what Christmas is either.

Clock: Could be - you are - right, Game.

Game: I suggest we relive that first Christmas many years ago to show O.S. and to serve as a refresher course for the rest of us. I guess toys can get wrapped up with the hustle and bustle just like people and forget the true meaning of the Christ of Christmas.

New Toy: Christmas?

Music Box: That's a great idea and we could have music and singing too. What's Christmas without music?

Ballerina: *(dancing around)* Music to dance to, I hope.

Raggedy Ann: Sh-h-h-h, Dancer. It's a fantastic idea and I'll bet Windy needs this refresher course the most. He is so mean all the time.

Woody: Just how do you propose to do this, Game?

Game: Since we are toys, we have the great power of imagination. All we have to do is concentrate on the same thing and, lo and behold, the scene of the first Christmas will appear right before our eyes. Understand?

New Toy: Christmas?

Jack: We can do it right here?

Game: No, we'd better do it in the back room in case the shopkeeper comes back.

Bear: Let's go! I'm anxious to see and hear about the first Christmas again.

New Toy: Christmas?

(As the toys leave the audience sings.)

Song: Silent Night, Holy Night *(Audience)*

> Silent night, holy night,
>   All is calm, all is bright
> Round yon virgin mother and child.
>   Holy infant so tender and mild,
> Sleep in heavenly peace,
> Sleep in heavenly peace.
>
> Silent night, holy night,
>   Shepherds quake at the sight,
> Glories stream from heaven afar,
>   Heavenly hosts sing alleluia;
> Christ, the Savior, is born!
> Christ, the Savior, is born!
>
> Silent night, holy night,
>   Son of God, love's pure light
> Radiant beams from thy holy face,
>   With the dawn of redeeming grace,
> Jesus, Lord, at thy birth,
> Jesus, Lord, at thy birth.
>   Joseph Mohr

Part Two

Cast

Announcer	Four shepherds
Mary	Herod
Joseph	Chief Priest and
Innkeeper	two other priests
Innkeeper's Daughter	Three Wise men
Angel	

Scene One

Announcer: The scene opens with all the toys concentrating with all their imaginative powers on the very first Christmas. You can see it is working as now an innkeeper can be seen at a table counting his money. This is a very busy time in Bethlehem for it is the time of the census and everyone belonging to the house of David must be in the city of their birth to be counted. That means the inns are filled with people returning for the count. Mary and Joseph are about to arrive.

(Mary and Joseph have been moving down the center aisle and should arrive as the announcer finishes speaking.)

Joseph: Mary, I'll try that inn over there next. I can see the innkeeper is right near the door.

Mary: I do hope you are successful in getting a room; I don't believe I can travel much longer, Joseph.

Joseph: Excuse me, sir. Would you have any room in your inn for my wife and me?

Innkeeper: Go away, young man. You must be crazy. All the rooms in town are filled. You are rather late, my dear fellow, to be searching for a room.

Joseph: I'm aware of that, but my wife is ill and we had to travel very slowly.

Innkeeper: I'm sorry to hear that, but there is nothing I can do. I have even rented out my own room.

Joseph: Thank you, anyway. *(turns to Mary)* I'm sorry. Mary, there is no room here either.

Mary: Oh, Joseph, what will we do? *(Joseph and Mary start to turn away)*

Daughter: Father, can't you see this woman is going to have a baby soon? We could at least give them a space in the stable.

Innkeeper: But, daughter, that's a place for animals, not people.

Daughter: In this situation I'm sure a place in the stable is better than nothing.

Innkeeper: Hey! Hey! you two, come back. You may have some space in the stable if you desire. It isn't much, but it is clean and warm.

Joseph: Thank you, kind sir. We will accept your offer as my wife must have a place to rest tonight.

Mary: Bless you and your family. We will be eternally grateful.

Innkeeper: Begone! I have much to do. My daughter will show you the way.

(Innkeeper goes off stage; daughter with Mary and Joseph go back to the stable, then the daughter leaves. The audience sings.)

Song: O Little Town of Bethlehem *(Audience)*

> O little town of Bethlehem,
>   How still we see thee lie!
> Above thy deep and dreamless sleep
>   The silent stars go by;
> Yet in thy dark streets shineth
>   The everlasting Light;
> The hopes and fears of all the years
>   Are met in thee tonight.
>
> For Christ is born of Mary,
>   And gathered all above,
> While mortals sleep, the angels keep
>   Their watch of wondering love.
> O morning stars, together

Proclaim the holy birth!
And praises sing to God the King,
    And peace to men on earth.

O holy Child of Bethlehem!
    Descend to us, we pray;
Cast out our sin and enter in;
    Be born in us today.
We hear the Christmas angels
    The great glad tidings tell;
O come to us, abide with us,
    Our Lord Emmanuel!

                                Phillips Brooks

Announcer: And so it was as the prophets predicted so many years before, that a Savior, a King, was born in a stable in Bethlehem. Jesus was born that night and Mary, his mother, wrapped him in swaddling clothes and laid him in a manger. It is hard for us to imagine that God's Son, our Savior, was born in a stable and that his bed was merely a place where the animals came to feed.

Song: Away in a Manger *(Children)*

Away in a manger, no crib for his bed,
    The little Lord Jesus laid down his sweet head.
The stars in the sky looked down where he lay,
    The little Lord Jesus asleep on the hay.

The cattle are lowing, the baby awakes,
    But little Lord Jesus, no crying he makes.
I love thee, Lord Jesus, look down from the sky,
    And stay by my cradle till morning is nigh.

                                Anonymous

Scene Two

Announcer: On this very same night, near Bethlehem, there were shepherds out in the fields keeping watch over their flocks to protect the sheep from harm.

Song: It Came Upon the Midnight Clear *(Audience)*

> It came upon the midnight clear,
>   That glorious song of old,
> From angels bending near the earth
>   To touch their harps of gold;
> "Peace on the earth, good will to men,
>   From heaven's all gracious King,"
> The world in solemn stillness lay
>   To hear the angels sing.
>   Edmund H. Sears

(Shepherds come down center aisle, during singing, and proceed up the steps during singing.)

Angel: *(comes from the side toward the shepherds who are frightened and drop to their knees and cover their eyes.)* "Fear not: for, behold, I bring you good tidings of great joy, which shall be to all people. For unto you is born this day in the city of David a Saviour, which is Christ the Lord. And this shall be a sign unto you; Ye shall find the babe wrapped in swaddling clothes, lying in a manger." (Luke 2:10–12)

Song: Hark! the Herald Angels Sing *(Audience)*

> Hark! the herald angels sing,
>   "Glory to the newborn King;
> Peace on earth, and mercy mild,
>   God and sinners reconciled."
> Joyful, all ye nations rise,
>   Join the triumph of the skies;
> With the angelic host proclaim,
>   "Christ is born in Bethlehem!"
> Hark! the herald angels sing,
>   "Glory to the newborn King!"
>   Charles Wesley

Shepherd One: Did you see that angel?

Shepherd Two: The light was so bright! It almost blinded me.

Shepherd Three: Did you hear what he said?

Shepherd One: Can you imagine? The angel said the Messiah was born right here in our own village of Bethlehem!

Shepherd Four: That's impossible! Why would an angel come to tell *us*? We are just shepherds.

Shepherd One: But you *did* see the angel, didn't you?

Shepherd Four: Y-y-y-es.

Shepherd Two: Remember our great king David was once a shepherd.

Shepherd Three: The prophets have said that the Promised One would come from the line of David.

Shepherd Four: That's right. They have always said that, and Bethlehem *is* the city of David.

Shepherd One: But I'm puzzled. Why would the new king be born in a stable?

Shepherd Three: Yes, that is strange. Seems like he would be born in a palace.

Shepherd Two: We shouldn't question, for each one of us heard the angel say we would find the newborn Savior in a manger.

Shepherd One: Let us move on to Bethlehem right now and see for ourselves if it is true.

Shepherd Four: What about our flocks?

Shepherd Two: I'm sure they will be all right, for this night is like no other we have seen or felt before!

Shepherd Three: Let us go directly to Bethlehem and see if we can find this new king the angel told us about.

(Shepherds proceed to the manger and kneel before the Christ child.)

Solo: What Child Is This?

> What child is this, who laid to rest,
> On Mary's lap is sleeping?
> Whom angels greet with anthems sweet,
> While shepherds watch are keeping?
>
> Refrain:
> This, this is Christ the King,
> Whom shepherds guard and angels sing:
> Haste, haste to bring him laud,
> The babe, the son of Mary.
>
>   William C. Dix

Scene Three

Announcer: About the same time the shepherds received the announcement of Christ's birth, another king, king Herod, was holding a meeting with some Jewish priests.

Herod: Priests, what is the meaning of this bright star?

First Priest: It is said that this exceptionally bright star in the East is leading the people to the birthplace of a new king who will rule the people of Israel.

Herod: Good, this should help the three wise men I sent to seek information on this so-called king, find him.

Second Priest: Do you think the wise men will return and pass the information on to you?

Herod: Of course, I am the king! How would they dare not to? Besides, I told them I wanted to know more about this new king so that I could go to worship him too.

First Priest: Do you believe he is the Messiah whom the Jews have been expecting for so many years?

Herod: I don't know, but I'm not taking any chances.

Second Priest: Does that mean you are not planning to honor him as you told the wise men?

Herod: Of course not! I must destroy him. He could be a threat to my power.

Chief Priest: I must caution you, Herod. This seems to fulfill the part of the prophecies from the prophet Micah. Here let me read this to you again, "But thou, Bethlehem Ephratah, though thou be little among the thousands of Judah, yet out of thee shall he come forth unto me that is to be ruler in Israel; whose goings forth have been from of old, from everlasting." (Micah 5:2)

Herod: Rubbish! I am the great king!

Announcer: The three wise men had left king Herod's palace without realizing the real reason Herod was so interested in this new King. As they left the palace they again saw the extraordinary bright star which had been their guide from their country far to the East. It now seemed to beckon them to follow it.

Scene Four

Song: We Three Kings of Orient Are *(Small group of children)*

> We three kings of Orient are,
>   Bearing gifts we traverse afar
> Field and fountain, moor and mountain,
>   Following yonder star.

Refrain:

> O star of wonder, star of night,
>   Star with royal beauty bright,
> Westward leading, still proceeding,
>   Guide us to thy perfect light.

Born a king on Bethlehem's plain,
  Gold I bring to crown him again,
King forever, ceasing never
  Over us all to reign.

Frankincense to offer have I,
  Incense owns a deity nigh;
Prayer and praising, all men raising,
  Worship him, God on high.

Myrrh is mine; its bitter perfume
  Breathes a life of gathering gloom:
Sorrowing, sighing, bleeding, dying,
  Sealed in the stone-cold tomb.

Glorious now behold him arise,
  King and God and Sacrifice;
Alleluia, alleluia!
  Sounds through the earth and skies.
                           John H. Hopkins, Jr.

(Wise men move down aisle during singing.)

First King: Why do you suppose Herod wanted us to find this king? Do you think he really wants to honor him?

Second King: I have my doubts, for if this baby is truly the Messiah-King, he would be a threat to Herod's position.

Third King: How do you suppose we will find this king? We know from Micah the prophet he will be in Bethlehem, but just where?

Second King: I have been watching the bright star we saw before we left home, and I believe it will lead us to the exact place where we will find the King of the Jews.

Third King: You are right, the star does seem to beckon us to follow its direction.

First King: Yes, it is shining right over the town of Bethlehem.

Third King: Look, the star is actually directly over that little house.

Second King: That's a sorry-looking abode for a king.

First King: It is not for us to judge where he is, but to bring him our gifts. You have them with you, don't you?

Second King: Yes, I brought gold.

Third King: I have myrrh.

First King: And I have frankincense.

Second King: Come, let us enter this house and make our visit to this King, the Savior of the world.

Announcer: The wise men went into the house and gave their gifts to the King, and left to tell Herod where he could be found. But that night they had a dream which warned them not to go to Herod. So the three wise men went another way to their own country. Meanwhile, Joseph also had a dream in which an angel came and told him that Herod planned to destroy their son Jesus. Joseph took Mary and Jesus and went to Egypt to live until it was safe to return.

Scene Five

Announcer: The toys in the shop have seen this enactment of the first Christmas. They now return to their original positions, and turn to the New Toy for his reaction.

Game: There, that is how the first Christmas came about.

Raggedy Ann: Do you understand now, O.S.?

New Toy: Go home! Christmas! Tell about Love!

Music Box: Wow! He does understand, and not a minute too soon. Here comes the shopkeeper!

(Toys freeze into position as the shopkeeper comes in and takes off his coat, hat, and gloves. He rubs his hands to warm them as he looks over all the toys.)

Song: Joy to the World *(Audience)*

Joy to the world! the Lord is come:
  Let earth receive her King;
Let every heart prepare him room,
  And heaven and nature sing.

Joy to the earth! the Savior reigns:
  Let men their songs employ;
While fields and floods, rocks, hills, and plains
  Repeat the sounding joy.

Isaac Watts

Written by Eileen Y. Carmer for the Sunday school of the Grandville-Jenison Congregational United Church of Christ, Grandville, Michigan.

6

Only Room in the Stable

Cast

Announcer	Lela
Four Readers	Job
Elisabeth	Ruth
Joshua	Jeb
Eve	Mary
Adam	Joseph
Miriam	Five Shepherds
Abraham	Three Kings

Reader One: "And it came to pass in those days, that there went out a decree from Caesar Augustus, that all the world should be taxed" (Luke 2:1). Caesar demanded that everyone must be taxed and counted in the city where their family originated. For many, this meant a long and tedious journey to the place of their ancestors.

Reader Two: "And Joseph also went up from Galilee, out of the city of Nazareth, into Judea, unto the city of David, which is called Bethlehem; (because he was of the house and lineage of David:) To be taxed with Mary his espoused wife, being great with child. And so it was, that, while they were there, the days were accomplished that she should be delivered" (Luke 2:4–6).

Reader Three: The story of Jesus' birth comes to us from

105

the Gospels of Luke and Matthew, but the story actually begins centuries earlier. It starts in the Garden of Eden when God said to Satan, "And I will put enmity between thee and the woman, and between thy seed and her seed; it shall bruise thy head, and thou shalt bruise his heel" (Gen. 3:15). The gospel was further proclaimed to Abraham, Isaac, and Jacob. The prophets of the Israelites not only proclaimed the power and majesty of the one true God, but they also told of his righteousness and love. They told of the coming of the Messiah who would free his people from their oppressors. Through all the Israelites' afflictions, this was their hope—the coming of the Messiah.

Reader Four: We shall try through this pageant to give something of the atmosphere of the time into which the Messiah was born; as well as something of the mystery, the simplicity, and the miracle of Christ's birth as told by Luke and Matthew.

(Exit Readers.)

Scene One

Announcer: The scene opens with a crowd of young people sitting in an inn in Bethlehem. Some are brothers and sisters, some cousins—all are related. They can be seen and heard discussing the day's events.

Lela: I don't know why my father is so mad that he has to come all the way back to Bethlehem to be counted and taxed. I think it's fun! No school, no chores, and we all get to see each other.

Job: All parents are the same. All they think about is the wasting of time and money.

Abraham: Why do we have to come to Bethlehem? Why can't we just pay our taxes in our own city?

Ruth: We have to come here because this is where our family first started.

Abraham: So!

Ruth: If your family is from the house of David, your family originated here in Bethlehem. We all are of David's lineage.

Job: Bethlehem is another name for the city of David.

Abraham: Who was David?

Elisabeth: Abraham, don't you know anything?

Lela: David is our ancestor from way back. He was one of our three famous kings. First there was Saul, then David, and then David's son, Solomon.

Job: That was back in the days when our people were free and not under the rule of any foreign country.

Abraham: Must have been better times than we have now.

Jeb: We have also come back to Bethlehem to be counted. See, if everyone is at the place they're supposed to be, it will make the census taking easier and more accurate.

Abraham: What is a census?

Elisabeth: You are a dummy, Abraham. Don't you go to school or synagogue in your city?

Abraham: Of course I go! Guess I don't pay much attention.

Jeb: Census is the process of numbering all the people and valuating their property for taxation.

Lela: Here come Joshua and Eve.

(Enter Joshua and Eve.)

Joshua: Wow! What a crowd in Bethlehem. There are people all over the place.

Eve: I'm sure glad we have relatives who own an inn so we knew we would have a place to stay.

Ruth: Did you see all the soldiers out and around too?

Eve: Aren't there always a lot of soldiers around to push, shove, and tell people what to do?

Ruth: But don't you think there are a lot more than usual?

Joshua: I'm sure there are, because there are more people.

Job: I imagine there are more soldiers to keep an eye on the tax collectors as king Herod trusts no one.

Elisabeth: That is a fact. King Herod trusts *no one*! I hear my parents discussing that often.

Eve: Just before we came in, we were talking to one of the watchmen and he said the entire city is full. All the inns and even the courtyards are full.

Jeb: Why don't the people sleep out in the fields as they often do?

Joshua: The watchman says everyone wants to be inside the walls, even if with only a blanket and the ground. Everyone is carrying money to pay their taxes and they feel more protected within the city.

Lela: When you arrived did you see Aaron, the old hermit from the hills?

Eve: Yes, we did.

Ruth: I suppose he is still chanting the words of the prophets to anyone who will listen to him?

Joshua: Yes, he is still proclaiming the birth of the Messiah.

Elisabeth: He believes the Messiah will come soon and end this tyranny of Rome, and the way of righteousness will rule our land.

Jeb: Do you think he is right? That the long-awaited Messiah will come soon?

Abraham: He can't arrive any too soon for me.

Joshua: We don't know when he will come, but we do know that some day it will happen.

Eve: Here come Adam and Miriam; they were just a little way behind us.

(Enter Adam and Miriam.)

Lela: What took you so long? It is just about time to call it a day.

Adam: Boy, it is sure a relief to finally get here. It is so slow traveling with little brothers and sisters. How such little people can slow you down, I will never know!

Miriam: It isn't all their fault. Traveling is very difficult, as the roads are rough and the hills are steep. Plus that, as we neared Bethlehem the passageways were crowded with all types of people.

Adam: There are soldiers, beggars, merchants, rich people, poor people, shepherds, sheep and other animals. You name it! They are here.

Miriam: We traveled a few days with Joseph, the carpenter from Nazareth, and his wife, Mary. They have a donkey for Mary to ride, but it is slow going as she is pregnant and expecting her baby soon, I would say.

Adam: We finally went ahead to get here before it got too dark. I don't know where they will ever get a room, the city looks rather full.

Job: Didn't they make arrangements for a room ahead of time?

Miriam: No, Joseph said that he hadn't realized it would take so long to get here. He expected to arrive a day or two ago.

Adam: In fact, Joseph was very concerned about where they would get a room, especially for Mary. I told him to check here at your father's inn.

Ruth: That will be a waste of time, as my father said the inn was full at noon already. But I'll go check and tell him about this situation. *(Ruth exits)*

Elisabeth: I sure don't know where they will stay. Look how crowded we will be tonight.

Eve: For us it will be fun and very little sleep.

Abraham: More fun if all you girls would leave or at least quit your gossiping and giggling.

Eve: How about boys! All you do is wrestle around and knock things over.

(Ruth returns.)

Ruth: I just helped my father place that couple in the stable, as he says there is definitely no room in the inn. This woman will have her baby soon and she desperately needed a place to rest. We just couldn't put her back out on the streets.

Miriam: That's the Mary and Joseph we traveled with?

Ruth: Yes, it is. They are from the house of David and are here for the census like the rest of us.

Lela: I feel sorry for them out in the stable. How awful to be with the animals.

Job: Hey, a stable is far from the worst place to be tonight. At least there is straw to rest on. The animals will keep it warm and best of all they will have privacy.

Jeb: Maybe we should offer to trade places.

Elisabeth: Better yet, let us all settle down for the night; there will be many things to do in the city tomorrow.

Joshua: That's right. There will be peddlers, merchants, sideshows, and all kinds of foods—lots and lots of good things to do and see. So let's get some sleep for the big day tomorrow.

(All lay down, say their prayers and goodnight. Lights out, frontstage.)

Song: Silent Night, Holy Night *(Audience)*

> Silent night, holy night,
>   All is calm, all is bright
> Round yon virgin mother and child.
>   Holy infant so tender and mild,
> Sleep in heavenly peace,
> Sleep in heavenly peace.
>
> Silent night, holy night,
>   Shepherds quake at the sight,
> Glories stream from heaven afar,
>   Heavenly hosts sing alleluia;
> Christ, the Savior, is born!
> Christ, the Savior, is born!
>
> Silent night, holy night,
>   Son of God, love's pure light
> Radiant beams from thy holy face,
>   With the dawn of redeeming grace,
> Jesus, Lord, at thy birth,
> Jesus, Lord, at thy birth.
>   Joseph Mohr

Scene Two

(Everyone on stage starts to stir and sit up.)

Adam: *(squinting)* What is giving off the bright light shining through the window?

Joshua: I don't know, but it sure makes it hard for a guy to sleep.

(Everyone goes to window.)

Miriam: *(pointing)* It's coming from a star!

Job: It looks like it is right above the stable.

Eve: In fact, it looks like it is shining right down on the stable and nowhere else.

Lela: I wonder why the star is shining so brightly tonight? It wasn't like that last night.

Elisabeth: What a wonderful, but scary sight.

Abraham: Sh! I hear a noise.

Ruth: What is it?

Abraham: I don't know, but it is getting closer.

Lela: I can hear voices and they sound excited.

Jeb: I can see what the commotion is. It is a bunch of shepherds coming over that hill. They are pointing to the star and to the stable.

Job: They seem to be heading to the stable.

Abraham: I wonder what's going on there?

Eve: That is where Mary and Joseph are.

Miriam: Do you think something has happened to them?

Adam: Why would the shepherds leave the fields in the middle of the night and come into the city?

Lela: I'm scared!

Abraham: You are always scared. It is only a bright star and a bunch of shepherds.

Job: How about we go to investigate?

Eve: You mean go out to the stable in the middle of the night?

Joshua: Yes, that is what he means. Hurry let's all go.

Ruth: Follow me, I know a shortcut to the stable.

(All the children get up and follow Ruth off stage.)

Song: O Little Town of Bethlehem *(Audience)*

> O little town of Bethlehem,
>   How still we see thee lie!
> Above thy deep and dreamless sleep
>   The silent stars go by;
> Yet in thy dark streets shineth
>   The everlasting Light;
> The hopes and fears of all the years
>   Are met in thee tonight.
>
> For Christ is born of Mary,
>   And gathered all above,
> While mortals sleep, the angels keep
>   Their watch of wondering love.
> O morning stars, together
>   Proclaim the holy birth!
> And praises sing to God the King,
>   And peace to men on earth.
>
> O holy Child of Bethlehem!
>   Descend to us, we pray;
> Cast out our sin and enter in;
>   Be born in us today.
> We hear the Christmas angels
>   The great glad tidings tell;

O come to us, abide with us,
Our Lord Emmanuel!

Phillips Brooks

Scene Three

(Children's choir sings "Away in a Manager." Joseph is standing behind Mary who is seated beside the manger in which Jesus is sleeping.)

Announcer: "And so it was, that, while they were there [in Bethlehem], the days were accomplished that she should be delivered. And she brought forth her firstborn son, and wrapped him in swaddling clothes, and laid him in a manger; because there was no room for them in the inn" (Luke 2:6–7).

Mary: Joseph, remember that we are to name this child Jesus?

Joseph: Yes, "For unto us a child is born, unto us a son is given. . . ."

Mary: He is so little and some day so much will be expected of him!

Joseph: Sh . . . It sounds like someone is coming.

Song: Hark! the Herald Angels Sing *(Audience)*

Hark! the herald angels sing,
   "Glory to the newborn King;
Peace on earth, and mercy mild,
   God and sinners reconciled!"
Joyful, all ye nations, rise,
   Join the triumph of the skies;
With the angelic host proclaim,
   "Christ is born in Bethlehem."

Refrain:
    Hark! the herald angels sing,
    "Glory to the newborn King!"

Christ, by highest heaven adored;
    Christ, the everlasting Lord!
Late in time behold him come,
    Offspring of the virgin's womb.
Veiled in flesh the Godhead see;
    Hail the incarnate deity,
Pleased as man with men to dwell,
    Jesus, our Emmanuel.

Hail the heavenborn Prince of peace!
    Hail the Sun of righteousness!
Light and life to all he brings,
    Risen with healing in his wings,
Mild he lays his glory by,
    Born that man no more may die,
Born to raise the sons of earth,
    Born to give them second birth.
                                    Charles Wesley

(During the last verse, shepherds come down the aisle and go up to the stage.)

Shepherd One: I sure have a hard time believing all this is really happening tonight.

Shepherd Two: You do see the star, don't you?

Shepherd One: Yes, I do. It is so bright!

Shepherd Three: It has guided us here and seems to be directly over that stable there. *(points)*

Shepherd Four: How about that angel that appeared to us? You agree you saw and heard that, don't you?

Shepherd One: Yes, but it is all so hard to believe!

Shepherd Five: It sure does all seem like a dream and we will wake up and be out in the fields watching over our flocks like we should be doing.

Shepherd Two: When the angel appeared in that blinding light I was so afraid!

Shepherd Three: We all dropped to our knees and covered our eyes.

Shepherd Five: Did you hear the music?

Shepherd Three: It sounded like a whole choir of voices.

Shepherd Four: Can you remember what the angel said?

Shepherd Two: I sure can! In fact, I doubt that I will ever forget it.

Shepherd One: Tell us again.

Shepherd Two: "Fear not: for, behold, I bring you good tidings of great joy, which shall be to all people. For unto you is born this day in the city of David a Saviour, which is Christ the Lord. And this shall be a sign unto you; Ye shall find the babe wrapped in swaddling clothes, lying in a manger." (Luke 2:10–12)

Shepherd Five: Can you really believe that the long-awaited Messiah would come to us as a baby, right here in the city of Bethlehem?

Shepherd Four: That seems possible, but that we are to find him in a *manger*!

Shepherd One: And why would an angel come announce it to us, shepherds?

Shepherd Two: We need to remember our great king David was once a shepherd from Bethlehem; the prophets for centuries have said that the Promised One would come from the line of David.

Shepherd Three: Why in a manger?

Shepherd Four: We shouldn't question why. I'm sure God has his reasons.

Shepherd Five: Look over there! The star is shining on that stable and seems to be telling us to end our journey there.

Shepherd Three: Let's go and visit our new King.

Shepherd Two: "Glory to God in the highest, and on earth peace, good will toward men" (Luke 2:14).

(Shepherds approach stable and bow down to the baby in the manger. Exit everyone.)

Scene Four

Song: We Three Kings of Orient Are *(Audience)*

> We three kings of Orient are,
>   Bearing gifts we traverse afar
> Field and fountain, moor and mountain,
>   Following yonder star.
>
> Refrain:
> O star of wonder, star of night,
>   Star with royal beauty bright,
> Westward leading, still proceeding,
>   Guide us to thy perfect light.
>
> Born a king on Bethlehem's plain,
>   Gold I bring to crown him again,
> King forever, ceasing never
>   Over us all to reign.
>
> Frankincense to offer have I,
>   Incense owns a deity nigh;
> Prayer and praising, all men raising,
>   Worship him, God on high.

Myrrh is mine; its bitter perfume
Breathes a life of gathering gloom:
Sorrowing, sighing, bleeding, dying,
Sealed in the stone-cold tomb.

Glorious now behold him arise,
King and God and Sacrifice;
Alleluia, alleluia!
Sounds through the earth and skies.

John H. Hopkins, Jr.

Announcer: "Now when Jesus was born in Bethlehem of Judea in the days of Herod the king, behold, there came wise men from the east to Jerusalem, Saying, Where is he that is born King of the Jews? for we have seen his star in the east, and are come to worship him. When Herod the king had heard these things, he was troubled, and all Jerusalem with him. And when he had gathered all the chief priests and scribes of the people together, he demanded of them where Christ should be born. And they said unto him, In Bethlehem of Judea. . . ." (Matt. 2:1–5)

(The three kings proceed down the aisle. Turn to face the audience.)

First King: Why do you suppose Herod told us to find this newborn king?

Second King: Do you think he really wants to come and honor this baby as he said?

Third King: I have my doubts, for if the long-awaited Messiah has really finally arrived, it would be nothing but trouble for Herod.

First King: I believe we have finally arrived in Bethlehem, the city which the prophet Micah proclaimed would be the birthplace of the Messiah.

Second King: That bright star in the East has guided us here. Now how can we find the home of this newborn king?

Third King: Look, the star has stopped right over that little house. Could that really be the place for a *king*?

Second King: That is not for us to decide. Come, we must pay him tribute with our gifts.

First King: I have brought gold as my gift for the new king.

Third King: I have frankincense to give him.

Second King: I brought myrrh.

First King: Come, let us see if this humble dwelling is where we will find the new Savior.

Second King: Let us worship him, and then decide what to do about going back to Herod.

(Exit kings.)

Announcer: "And when they were come into the house, they saw the young child with Mary his mother, and fell down, and worshipped him: and when they had opened their treasures, they presented unto him gifts; gold, and frankincense, and myrrh. And being warned of God in a dream that they should not return to Herod, they departed into their own country another way." (Matt. 2:11–12).

Reader One: Isaiah's prophecy has been fulfilled: "For unto us a child is born, unto us a son is given: and the government shall be upon his shoulder: and his name shall be called Wonderful, Counsellor, the mighty God, the everlasting Father, the Prince of Peace." (Isa. 9:6)

Song: Joy to the World *(Audience)*

> Joy to the world! the Lord is come:
> Let earth receive her King;

Let every heart prepare him room,
  And heaven and nature sing,
  And heaven and nature sing,
  And heaven, and heaven and nature sing.

Joy to the earth! the Savior reigns:
  Let men their songs employ;
While fields and floods, rocks, hills, and plains
  Repeat the sounding joy,
  Repeat the sounding joy,
  Repeat, repeat the sounding joy.

He rules the world with truth and grace,
  And makes the nations prove
The glories of his righteousness,
  And wonders of his love,
  And wonders of his love,
  And wonders, wonders of his love

                            Isaac Watts

Written by Eileen Y. Carmer for the Sunday School of the Grandville-Jenison Congregational United Church of Christ, Grandville, Michigan.

7

Messenger of Peace

(Spotlights focused on choir pews and narrator. Sanctuary lights dim. Choir enters humming "Silent Night." Congregation sings stanza 3 when choir is in place. All lights out except spot on narrator when carol is finished.)

Narrator: "And there were in the same country shepherds abiding in the field, keeping watch over their flocks by night. And, lo, the angel of the Lord came upon them, and the glory of the Lord shone round about them: and they were sore afraid. And the angel said unto them, Fear not: for, behold, I bring you good tidings of great joy, which shall be to all people. For unto you is born this day in the city of David a Saviour, which is Christ the Lord" (Luke 2:8–11).

(Choir lights come on.)

Choir: "Glory to God in the Highest" —G. B. Pergolesi

Narrator: "Glory to God in the highest, and on earth peace, good will toward men" (Luke 2:14). The angels in heaven were singing his praises and the shepherds on earth rejoiced. God's Son in human flesh had come to earth. But why was it necessary for Christ to come to earth? He came to die on a cross to save man from eternal damnation. He was born of a virgin and became like man except in sin.

Song: Good Christian Men, Rejoice *(Audience)*

> Good Christian men, rejoice,
>   With heart and soul and voice;
> Give ye heed to what we say:
>   Jesus Christ is born today;
> Ox and ass before him bow,
>   And he is in the manger now.
>   Christ is born today!
>   Christ is born today!
>
> Good Christian men, rejoice,
>   With heart and soul and voice;
> Now ye hear of endless bliss;
>   Jesus Christ was born for this!
> He hath oped the heavenly door,
>   And man is blessed evermore.
>   Christ was born for this!
>   Christ was born for this!
>
> Good Christian men, rejoice,
>   With heart and soul and voice;
> Now ye need not fear the grave;
>   Jesus Christ was born to save!
> Calls you one and calls you all,
>   To gain his everlasting hall.
>   Christ was born to save!
>   Christ was born to save!
>   German-Latin Carol
>   Tr. John M. Neale

(Two men stand on platform with spotlights focused on them. Rest of platform is dark. First man knocks on wood three times—silence—knocks three more times, much louder.)

Second Man: Stop that racket! What's this noise all about?

First Man: Sir! Sir, do you have a room available?

Second Man: No, everybody's coming to pay their taxes

and I haven't got one room left. Now go away and be quiet!

First Man: But sir! My wife is pregnant and the baby is coming very soon!

Second Man: Oh, you crazy young people! All right, you may use the stable.   '

First Man: The stable! But the baby is about to be born.

Second Man: The stable is all I have. It's around back—now goodnight!

(Spotlights switch to choir and men exit platform.)

Song: Thou Didst Leave Thy Throne *(Choir)*

> Thou didst leave thy throne and thy kingly crown
>   When thou camest to earth for me,
> But in Bethlehem's home there was found no room
>   For thy holy nativity.
> O come to my heart, Lord Jesus;
> There is room in my heart for thee!
>
> Heaven's arches rang when the angels sang,
>   Proclaiming thy royal degree,
> But in lowly birth didst thou come to earth,
>   And in great humility.
> O come to my heart, Lord Jesus;
> There is room in my heart for thee!
>
> Emily E. S. Elliott

Narrator: Jesus was born of a virgin in the humblest of circumstances. He was born in a stable and laid in a manger. And yet despite these humble circumstances, his very being radiated his kingship. Men, women, and children love to sing songs about Jesus, the Babe in the manger.

(Platform lights dim, Mary and Joseph come and sit by the manger. Spotlight on manger scene.)

124 Christmas Programs

Solo: What Child Is This?

What child is this, who laid to rest,
  On Mary's lap is sleeping?
Whom angels greet with anthems sweet,
  While shepherds watch are keeping?

Refrain:
This, this is Christ the King,
  Whom shepherds guard and angels sing:
Haste, haste to bring him laud,
  The babe, the son of Mary.
William C. Dix

(Junior choir enters from rear of sanctuary singing "Away in the Manger." They gather around the manger and finish their song.)

Song: Never Shone a Light So Fair *(Junior Choir)*

Never shone a light so fair,
  Never fell so sweet a song,
As the chorus in the air,
  Chanted by the angel-throng;
Every star took up the story,
  "Christ has come, the Prince of glory,
Come in humble hearts to dwell,
  God with us, God with us.
God with us, Immanuel."

Welcome now the blessed day
  When we praise the Lord our King;
When we meet to praise and pray,
  And his love with gladness sing;
Let the world take up the story,
  "Christ has come, the Prince of glory,
Come in humble hearts to dwell,
  God with us, God with us,
God with us, Immanuel."
Fanny Crosby

Narrator: *(in cadence with pianist)*

Humble praises, holy Jesus,
Children's voices raise to thee.
In thy mercy, oh, receive us!
Suffer us thy lambs to be.

Refrain:
Hallelujah, sweetly singing,
Joyful tribute now we bring.
Hallelujah, Hallelujah!
Hallelujah to our King.

Gracious Savior, be thou with us;
Let thy mercy richly flow.
Give thy Spirit, blessed Jesus;
Light and life on us bestow.
                    Author Unknown

(Piano fades out.)

Narrator: For his only son, born to Mary, God chose the
name *Jesus*. Transliterated from the Hebrew form,
Yehoshuah, Jesus means "Yahweh is salvation." It is such
a beautiful and precious name.

(Platform lights back to full)

Choir: Jesus, Priceless Treasure *(stanza 3)*

Banished is our sadness!
For the Lord of gladness,
Jesus, enters in.
Those who love the Father,
Though the storms may gather,
Still have peace within.
Yea, whate'er we here must bear,
Still in Thee lies purest pleasure,
Jesus, priceless treasure!
            Johann Franck
            Tr. Catherine Winkworth

(Spotlights on two men sitting in chairs on platform. Rest of platform is dark.)

First Man: Isn't Christmas a wonderful time of the year?

Second Man: *(cynically)* What's so great about it?

First Man: Well, everyone seems so happy and friendly.

Second Man: If you mean the merchants and business people. Wouldn't you be friendly too if you were making a lot of money from Christmas sales?

First Man: No! I mean there seems to be a general feeling of love and good will.

Second Man: I don't agree. Man is basically self-centered. He is only interested in helping himself—even at Christmas.

First Man: But that's just why we celebrate Christmas. Jesus came into a self-centered, sinful world to save people from their sins. And he has reached into the hearts of men and women and changed their lives. That's where Christmas is really celebrated—in the hearts of those who love Jesus.

(Spotlights out, men remain on chairs.)

Narrator: Yes, Christmas is celebrated in the heart and we as Christians have many favorite Christmas carols to express the love and joy which is in our hearts.

(Sanctuary lights come on and audience joins the choirs in singing a number of familiar carols.)

Audience and choirs: (Familiar carols such as those listed below.)

  "It Came Upon the Midnight Clear"
  "Hark, the Herald Angels Sing"

"O Come, All Ye Faithful"

"Joy to the World"

(Sanctuary lights dim.)

Narrator: Love! Love! God chose one of the most difficult ways to express his love for mankind. He gave his only Son. We celebrate Christmas because, nearly two thousand years ago, Jesus came to earth. When God sent Jesus as a baby to be born of a virgin he showed beyond any doubt the great love he had for his people.

(Spotlights on choir.)

Choir: "What Wondrous Love Is This?"

(Spotlights switch from choir to two men in chairs.)

Narrator: God sent Jesus into the world that we might have inward peace. By believing and trusting in Him, we can be free of inward strife.

Second Man: Just a minute now! If it is true that Jesus came as a Messenger of Peace, why is there so much hate in the world? And why all the wars and rumors of wars?

First Man: Mankind as a whole has not accepted this perfect gift of love—Jesus Christ. However, each year as Christians around the world celebrate Christmas, there is renewed hope that the perfect peace which God offers through his Son, Jesus, will be accepted by people of all nations.

(Men exit platform.)

Song: Savior of the Nations, Come *(Audience and Choirs)*

Savior of the nations, come,
Virgin's son, make here thy home!

Marvel now, O heaven and earth,
    That the Lord chose such a birth.

Not of flesh and blood the Son,
    Offspring of the Holy One;
Born of Mary ever blest
    God in flesh is manifest.

Wondrous birth! O wondrous child
    Of the virgin undefiled!
Though by all the world disowned,
    Still to be in heaven enthroned.

From the Father forth he came
    And returneth to the same,
Captive leading death and hell,
    High the song of triumph swell!

Thou, the Father's only Son,
    Hast o'er sin the victory won.
Boundless shall thy kingdom be;
    When shall we its glories see?

Praise to God the Father sing,
    Praise to God the Son, our King,
Praise to God the Spirit be
    Ever and eternally.

                              Ambrose of Milan

Narrator: Christmas! What does it mean to you? Is it a time
for decorations and good food? Is it a time when the family
gathers for a yearly get-together? Is it a time for giving and
receiving gifts? Christmas can be all of these things, but it
should be so much more! It should be a time of celebrating
God's gift to the world. It should be a time when we renew
our love for our fellow men. It should be a time when peace
is renewed within our hearts.

(Spotlights on choir.)

Choir: Now Let Every Tongue Adore Thee
            Glory to God in the Highest

Written by Jan and Virgil Leatherman for the Orchard View Church of God,
Grand Rapids, Michigan. Given Christmas, 1978.

8

O Come, All Ye Faithful

Cast

Puppets—
Church mice
  Minnie
  Gramps
Eve
Abraham
Moses
Ruth

David
John the Baptist
Seven Prophets
Three Readers
Four Shepherds
Three Wise Men

(Children sing two stanzas of "O Come, All Ye Faithful" in a processional to the stage. They sing the last stanza after the adult leader's opening prayer. The children exit from stage and the puppets take their places.)

Song: O Come, All Ye Faithful

> O come, all ye faithful, joyful and triumphant,
>   O come ye, O come ye to Bethlehem;
> Come and behold him, born the King of angels;
>
> Refrain:
> O come, let us adore him,
> O come, let us adore him,
> O come, let us adore him,
> Christ, the Lord!

Sing, choirs of angels, sing in exultation,
  Sing, all ye citizens of heaven above!
Glory to God, all glory in the highest;

Yea, Lord, we greet thee, born this happy morning,
  Jesus, to thee be all glory given;
Word of the Father, now in flesh appearing;
                                        John F. Wade
                                        Tr. Frederick Oakeley

Minnie: Not this again!

Gramps: What do you mean?

Minnie: The same song, the same program, year after year. This is my third Christmas in this church and I keep hearing the same thing!

Gramps: Minnie! For shame! It's the birthday of Jesus and I've heard this celebration for years—I've lost count of how many. I never get tired of Christmas concerts.

Minnie: You must be one of those faithful ones. I just don't feel that joyful or triumphant.

Gramps: Take it from one who has been around a little longer than you Minnie; the more I heard of Christmas, the more I wanted to hear. That's why these parents start bringing the little ones to Sunday school at such an early age. I should have started you earlier.

Minnie: Do you really think those littlest children are getting anything out of this?

Gramps: Sure do! Listen, let's hear for ourselves what they've got to say. Here come Matthew, Nicholas, Laura, Natasha, Breann, and Tricia.

(Substitute actual names of nursery school class.)

(Nursery class goes on stage and sings "Happy Christmas Bells" or another appropriate song, then exits to pews. Pianist continues to play until all are seated.)

Minnie: My, that was sweet. But I still don't understand how anyone can feel so triumphant and loving about a man named Jesus.

Gramps: If you would listen, and not ask so many questions you could find out. It happened a long, long time ago—many, many years before I was born. Oh, I better listen because some people older than I are coming to tell us about it.

(An appropriate scene can be projected on an overhead screen as each Old Testament character steps forward to the microphone to give his/her message.)

Eve: I am Eve, the first woman. Adam and I sinned when we were in the Garden of Eden. God loved us and promised to send a Savior who would destroy Satan and save us from eternal death. God said to Satan, the serpent, "I will put enmity between thee and the woman, and between thy seed and her seed; it shall bruise thy head, and thou shalt bruise his heel" (Gen. 3:15).

Abraham: My name is Abraham. Nearly twenty-five years before Sarah and I had a son, God told me the Savior would be born from my family. Sarah, my wife, was over ninety years old when God worked the miracle of Isaac's birth. God said to me, "I will make of thee a great nation, and I will bless thee, and make thy name great; and thou shalt be a blessing" (Gen. 12:2).

Moses: My name is Moses. God gave me and my people his perfect Law to teach us how to live, but we continually disobeyed. God always forgave us and promised to send us a Savior who would be a prophet-teacher. He said, "I will raise them up a Prophet from among their brethren, like unto thee, and will put my words in his mouth; and he shall speak unto them all that I shall command him" (Deut. 18:18).

Ruth: I am Ruth the Moabitess. I chose to follow the peo-

ple of God. I said to my mother-in-law, Naomi,
". . . whither thou goest, I will go; and where thou
lodgest, I will lodge: thy people shall be my people, and
thy God my God" (Ruth 1:16). God blessed me, and made
me the great, great grandmother of king David.

David: My name is David. When the prophet Samuel came
to my house to anoint a king in the place of Saul, my father
was sure that my older, more handsome brother, Eliab
would be chosen. But the Lord said, ". . . the Lord seeth
not as man seeth; for man looketh on the outward ap-
pearance, but the Lord looketh on the heart" (1 Sam.
16:7). So I was chosen to be king over Israel and from my
descendants the Christ child was born.

Song: O Come, O Come, Emmanuel *(Audience)*

O come, O come, Emmanuel,
  And ransom captive Israel,
That mourns in lonely exile here
  Until the Son of God appear.

Refrain:
Rejoice! Rejoice! Emmanuel shall come to thee, O Israel.

O come, thou branch of Jesse's stem,
  Unto thine own, and rescue them!
From depths of hell thy people save,
  And give them victory o'er the grave.

O come, thou Bright and Morning Star,
  And bring us comfort from afar!
Dispel the shadows of the night,
  And turn our darkness into light.

Anonymous Latin Hymn
Tr. John Mason Neale

*(During the singing the Old Testament characters exit the
stage and the prophets enter together. Each prophet steps
forward to the microphone to give his/her message.)*

Gramps: Listen carefully, Minnie; hear what these wise prophets have to say.

Minnie: My! Look how they are dressed. They are sure out of it!

First Prophet: We are the prophets who foretold the Messiah's coming—that Jesus would be born. We weren't very popular because we told the Israelites they must repeat of their sins. The people didn't listen to us and God punished them by sending them into exile for many years.

Isaiah: I am Isaiah. "For unto us a child is born, unto us a son is given: and the government shall be upon his shoulder: and his name shall be called Wonderful, Counsellor, The mighty God, The everlasting Father, The Prince of Peace. Of the increase of his government and peace there shall be no end . . ." (Isa. 9:6, 7).

Jeremiah: I am Jeremiah. "Behold the days come, saith the LORD, that I will make a new covenant with the house of Israel, and with the house of Judah: Not according to the covenant that I made with their fathers . . . But this shall be the covenant . . . I will put my law in their inward parts, and write it in their hearts; and will be their God, and they shall be my people" (Jer. 31:31–33).

Ezekiel: I am Ezekiel. "For thus saith the Lord GOD; Behold, I, even I, will both search my sheep, and seek them out. As a shepherd seeketh out his flock . . . that are scattered; so will I seek out my sheep, and will deliver them out of all places where they have been scattered . . . And I will set up one shepherd over them, and he shall feed them, even my servant David; he shall feed them, and he shall be their shepherd" (Ezek. 34:11, 12, 23).

Daniel: I am Daniel. "I saw . . . and, behold, one like the Son of man came with the clouds of heaven, and came to the Ancient of days, and they brought him near before him. And there was given him dominion, and glory, and a kingdom, that all people, nations, and languages, should serve him: his dominion is an everlasting dominion, which shall not pass away, and his kingdom that which shall not be destroyed" (Dan. 7:13, 14).

Micah: I am Micah. "But thou, Bethlehem Ephratah, though thou be little among the thousands of Judah, yet out of thee shall he come forth unto me that is to be ruler in Israel; whose goings forth have been from of old, from everlasting" (Mic. 5:2).

Zechariah: I am Zechariah. "Rejoice greatly, O daughter of Zion; shout, O daughter of Jerusalem: behold, thy King cometh unto thee: he is just, and having salvation; lowly and riding upon an ass, and upon a colt the foal of an ass" (Zech. 9:9).

John the Baptist: God sent me, John the Baptist, to prepare the way for the Savior's coming. My father, Zacharias, was a priest. One time when he was serving in the temple of the Lord, the angel Gabriel came to him and told him that he and my mother Elisabeth would have a son. They were to name him John. He didn't believe Gabriel because both he and my mother were very old and had given up all hope of ever having a child. Because he doubted God's promise he was unable to speak from that time until I was born. My work on earth was to tell people to repent of their sins and be baptized.

(Grades five, six, seven, and eight sing the chorus of "O come, O Come, Emmanuel.")

> Rejoice! Rejoice!
> Emmanuel
> Shall come to thee,
> O Israel.

Song: Come, Thou Long-expected Jesus *(Audience)*

Come, thou long-expected Jesus,
   Born to set thy people free;
From our fears and sins release us;
   Let us find our rest in thee.

Israel's strength and consolation,
   Hope of all the earth thou art;
Dear desire of every nation,
   Joy of every longing heart.

Born thy people to deliver,
   Born a Child and yet a King,
Born to reign in us forever,
   Now thy gracious kingdom bring.

By thine own eternal Spirit
   Rule in all our hearts alone;
By thine all-sufficient merit
   Raise us to thy glorious throne.
                       Charles Wesley

(During the singing of this song the prophets exit. Enter the three Readers.)

Reader One: When the time came for Jesus to come to earth, God sent the angel Gabriel to Mary, a young lady who lived in the village of Nazareth.

Reader Two: When Mary saw the angel she was afraid, but Gabriel said, "Fear not, Mary: for thou hast found favour with God. And, behold, thou shalt conceive . . . and bring forth a son, and shalt call his name JESUS. He shall be great, and shall be called the Son of the Highest: and the Lord God shall give unto him the throne of his father David: And he shall reign over the house of Jacob for ever; and of his kingdom there shall be no end" (Luke 1:30–33).

Reader Three: Soon after that Mary went to share her good news with her cousin Elisabeth who would soon become the mother of John the Baptist. While there Mary sang a beautiful song of praise to God for her Son who would become the Savior of the world.

All Three Readers: *(If you have a soloist who can sing the Magnificat it would be effective at this point.)*

> My soul doth magnify the Lord, and my spirit hath rejoiced in God my Savior.
> For he hath regarded the low estate of his handmaiden: for, behold, from henceforth all generations shall call me blessed.
> For he that is mighty hath done to me great things; and holy is his name.
> And his mercy is on them that fear him from generation to generation.
> He hath shewed strength with his arm; he hath scattered the proud in the imagination of their hearts.
> He hath put down the mighty from their seats, and exalted them of low degree.
> He hath filled the hungry with good things; and the rich he hath sent empty away . . ." (Luke 1:46–53).

Reader One: "And it came to pass in those days, that there went out a decree from Caesar Augustus, that all the world should be taxed . . . And all went to be taxed, every one to his own city. And Joseph also went up from Galilee out of the city of Nazareth, into Judea, unto the city of David, which is called Bethlehem . . . To be taxed with Mary his espoused wife, being great with child. And so it was, that, while they were there, the days were accomplished that she should be delivered. And she brought forth her firstborn son, and wrapped him in swaddling clothes, and laid him in a manger; because there was no room for them in the inn" (Luke 2:1–7).

(While the stage is being set with the manger scene, the pianist plays "Away in a Manger." Mary is kneeling down at the cradle and Joseph is standing beside her. The nursery class comes on stage and gathers around Mary and Joseph and sings "Away in a Manger.")

Minnie: Was he really born in a manger, a cattle shed?

Gramps: Yes, and his first visitors were poor shepherds.

Reader Three: "And there were in the same country shepherds abiding in the field, keeping watch over their flock by night. And, lo, the angel of the Lord came upon them, and the glory of the Lord shone round about them: and they were sore afraid. And the angel said to them,

Reader Two: "Fear not: for, behold, I bring you good tidings of great joy, which shall be to all people. For unto you is born this day in the city of David, a Saviour, which is Christ the Lord. And this shall be a sign unto you; Ye shall find the babe wrapped in swaddling clothes, lying in a manger.

Reader One: "And suddenly there was with the angel a multitude of the heavenly host praising God, and saying,

All Three Readers: "Glory to God in the highest, and on earth peace, good will toward men" (Luke 2:8–14).

(Enter shepherds)

First Shepherd: When we saw the angel and the bright light we were so scared we couldn't move!

Second Shepherd: You should have heard the joyful song which was sung by a whole chorus of angels! It was as if we could see right into heaven.

Third Shepherd: It was as if all of us were dreaming the same dream.

Fourth Shepherd: We couldn't wait to find out if what the angel told us was true, and here we find everything just like he said.

(The shepherds kneel and worship the Christ child.)

Minnie: Did Jesus come just for poor people like the shepherds?

Gramps: O no, Minnie. While Mary and Joseph were still in Bethlehem some wise, rich kings came from a far-eastern country to worship Jesus too.

(The wise men enter with their gifts for Jesus.)

First Wise Man: We came from a country far to the East with gifts for this new child King who was born.

Second Wise Man: We saw his star in the East and it guided us to the very place where Jesus was born. I offer to him my gift of gold.

Third Wise Man: We traveled a long way, but have found him who is to be King of kings. I give him my gift of myrrh.

First Wise Man: We have found this wonderful Babe, not in a palace, but in a lowly dwelling place. I give him my gift of sweet-smelling frankincense.

Song: What Can I Give Him? *(All those on stage)*

> What can I give him,
>   Poor as I am?
> If I were a shepherd,
>   I would bring a lamb;
> If I were a wise man,
>   I would do my part;
> Yet what I can I give him—
>   Give my heart.
>   Christina G. Rossetti

Adult Leader: The best gift we can give to Jesus our Savior is our love. We show our love to him by helping others. Our offering today is for those who do not have enough to eat and drink. Jesus said that if we give to others who are in need it is the same as giving to him.

(It might be quite meaningful if the children were told in advance to bring gifts for needy children which they had purchased, made or given from their own possessions.)

Song: We Give Thee but Thine Own *(Audience)*

> We give thee but thine own,
> Whate'er the gift may be;
> All that we have is thine alone,
> A trust, O Lord, from thee.

Minnie: Now I see what you mean. That was beautiful! Now I feel joyful and triumphant too.

Gramps: These Christmas concerts always leave me speechless!

Minnie: I think those little children really do understand about Jesus coming to the world as a baby and a King. I sure would like to hear everyone sing "O Come, All Ye Faithful." This time I'll sing along too.

Song: O Come, All Ye Faithful *(Audience)*

> O come, all ye faithful, joyful and triumphant,
>   O come ye, O come ye to Bethlehem;
> Come and behold him, born the King of angels;
>
> Refrain:
> O come, let us adore him,
> O come, let us adore him,
> O come, let us adore him,
> Christ, the Lord!
>
> Sing, choirs of angels, sing in exultation,
>   Sing, all ye citizens of heaven above!
> Glory to God, all glory in the highest;
>
> Yea, Lord, we greet thee, born this happy morning,
>   Jesus, to thee be all glory given;
> Word of the Father, now in flesh appearing;
>   John F. Wade
>   Tr. Frederick Oakeley

(During the singing of the last stanza the children's choir quietly assembles on stage)

Songs: Once in Royal David's City *(Children's Choir)*

>   Once in royal David's city
>   Stood a lowly cattle shed,
>   Where a mother laid her baby
>   In a manger for his bed.
>   Mary was that mother mild,
>   Jesus Christ her little child.
>
>   He came down to earth from heaven
>   Who is God and Lord of all,
>   And his shelter was a stable,
>   And his cradle was a stall.
>   With the poor, the mean, the lowly,
>   Lived on earth our Savior holy.
>
>   Not in that poor lowly stable
>   With the oxen standing by,
>   Shall we see him, but in heaven,
>   Set at God's right hand on high,
>   When like stars his children crowned
>   All in white shall wait around.
>
>   Cecil F. Alexander

Thou Didst Leave Thy Throne

>   Thou didst leave thy throne and thy kingly crown
>   When thou camest to earth for me,
>   But in Bethlehem's home there was found no room
>   For thy holy nativity.
>   O come to my heart, Lord Jesus;
>   There is room in my heart for thee!
>
>   Heaven's arches rang when the angels sang,
>   Proclaiming thy royal degree,
>   But in lowly birth didst thou come to earth,
>   And in great humility.
>   O come to my heart, Lord Jesus:
>   There is room in my heart for thee!
>
>   Emily E.S. Elliott

This program was adapted from one written by Elaine Bruxvoort for the Hope Christian Reformed Church of Stony Plain, Alberta, Canada given Christmas, 1984.

9

An Old-Fashioned Christmas

Cast

Narrator	Two Innkeepers
Child	Five Readers
Angel	Shepherds
Mary	Three Wise Men
Joseph	

(Enter Narrator and Child.)

Narrator: I can recall Christmas programs of years gone by. Grandpas and grandmas, aunts and uncles sat smiling in the sanctuary. Nervous, fidgety boys and girls were up in front watched by equally nervous but proud moms and dads. These programs were special because they were services of worship and praise led by the children. The program would always begin with a welcome speech by one of the tiny tots.

Child:

Welcome! Welcome, everyone!
We're glad that you could come.
Together we can sing and pray
And thank our God today
For sending us his Son.

Narrator: The wonderful story of Jesus' birth is retold each year. Generations of boys and girls learn of how God sent his Son into the world to save us from sin. With minds full of wonder, they try to imagine how it all happened.

(Mary and Angel enter. Child exits.)

Angel: "Hail, thou that art highly favoured, the Lord is with thee: blessed art thou among women. . . . Fear not, Mary: for thou hast found favour with God. And, behold, thou shalt conceive in thy womb, and bring forth a son, and shalt call his name JESUS. He shall be great, and shall be called the Son of the Highest: and the Lord God shall give unto him the throne of his father David: And he shall reign over the house of Jacob for ever; and of his kingdom there shall be no end" (Luke 1:28, 30–33).

(Angel exits)

Solo: My Soul Doth Magnify the Lord (The Magnificat)

(Mary exits. Enter Readers.)

Reader One: "And it came to pass in those days, that there went out a decree from Caesar Augustus, that all the world should be taxed.

Reader Two: "(And this taxing was first made when Cyrenius was governor of Syria.)

Reader Three: "And all went to be taxed, every one into his own city.

Reader Four: "And Joseph also went up from Galilee, out of the city of Nazareth, into Judea, unto the city of David, which is called Bethlehem; (because he was of the house and lineage of David:)

Reader Five: "To be taxed with Mary his espoused wife, being great with child" (Luke 2:1–5).

(Joseph, Mary and Innkeepers enter.)

Narrator: Joseph and Mary searched and searched in the crowded little town of Bethlehem for a place to stay. How discouraging it must have been to be told, "There is no room for you."

Joseph: *(Knocks on door and innkeeper opens it.)* Please, we need a place to stay.

First Innkeeper: We're all filled up tonight. Didn't you see the "No Vacancy" sign? *(slams door)*

(Joseph leads Mary to the door where he knocks again.)

Second Innkeeper: Sorry, no room!

Joseph: Please! We must have a place to stay tonight. Don't you have any place for us?

Second Innkeeper: *(scratches his head and finally points to the stable)* Over there, you may use one of the mangers.

(Mary and Joseph take places in manger scene. Innkeeper exits.)

Narrator: And so it was that the holy event took place. God's only Son was born in a stable!

Reader Five: "And she brought forth her firstborn son, and wrapped him in swaddling clothes, and laid him in a manger, because there was no room for them in the inn" (Luke 2:7).

(Children return to their seats.)

Reader One: "And there were in the same country shepherds abiding in the field, keeping watch over their flock by night.

Reader Two: "And, lo, the angel of the Lord came upon them, and the glory of the Lord shone round about them: and they were sore afraid.

Reader Three: "And the angel said unto them, Fear not: for, behold, I bring you good tidings of great joy, which shall be to all people.

Reader Four: "For unto you is born this day in the city of David, a Saviour, which is Christ the Lord.

Reader Five: "And this shall be a sign unto you; Ye shall find the babe wrapped in swaddling clothes, lying in a manger.

Reader One: "And suddenly there was with the angel a multitude of the heavenly host praising God, and saying,

All Readers: "Glory to God in the highest, and on earth peace, good will toward men" (Luke 2:8–14).

Narrator: Try to imagine the night sky filled with shining angels! What an amazing sight that must have been when the wonderful news of the birth of the King was first told to those humble shepherds. No wonder they hurried to Bethlehem to see what the Lord had done.

(Shepherds enter and assume a position of worship at the manger.)

Song: Angels, From the Realms of Glory *(Audience)*

> Angels, from the realms of glory,
>   Wing your flight o'er all the earth;
> Ye who sang creation's story,
>   Now proclaim Messiah's birth:
>   Come and worship, come and worship,
>   Worship Christ, the newborn King.
>
> Shepherds, in the field abiding,
>   Watching o'er your flocks by night,
> God with man is now residing;

Yonder shines the infant Light:
Come and worship, come and worship,
Worship Christ, the newborn King.

Sages, leave your contemplations,
    Brighter visions beam afar;
Seek the great Desire of nations;
    Ye have seen his natal star:
Come and worship, come and worship,
Worship Christ, the newborn King.

Saints, before the altar bending,
    Watching long in hope and fear,
Suddenly the Lord, descending,
    In his temple shall appear:
Come and worship, come and worship,
Worship Christ, the newborn King.
                                James Montgomery

(Children from grades one and two assemble on stage during the singing of the last stanza.)

Song: Away in a Manger *(First and Second Graders)*

Away in a manger, no crib for His bed,
    The little Lord Jesus lay down his sweet head;
The stars in the heavens looked down where he lay,
    The little Lord Jesus asleep in the hay.

The cattle are lowing, the baby awakes,
    But little Lord Jesus, no crying he makes;
I love thee, Lord Jesus, look down from the sky,
    And stay by my cradle till morning is nigh.

Be near me, Lord Jesus! I ask thee to stay
    Close by me forever, and love me, I pray.
Bless all the dear children in thy tender care.
    And take us to heaven to live with thee there.
                                Anonymous

(Children return to their seats.)

Narrator: What a special baby this was! He was not an ordinary child. The baby Jesus was the very Son of God! Mary and Joseph knew it. As Mary looked at Jesus she must have wondered, "What Child Is This?" The words of the song capture a mingling of joy and sorrow that God's Son was born to die. Listen as the girls sing.

Song: What Child Is This? *(All girls)*

> What child is this, who laid to rest,
>   On Mary's lap is sleeping?
> Whom angels greet with anthems sweet,
>   While shepherds watch are keeping?
>
> Refrain:
>
> This, this is Christ the King,
>   Whom shepherds guard and angels sing:
> Haste, haste, to bring him laud,
>   The babe, the son of Mary.
>
> So bring him incense, gold, and myrrh,
>   Come peasant, king, to own him;
> The King of kings salvation brings,
>   Let loving hearts enthrone him.
>   William C. Dix

Narrator: "So bring him incense, gold and myrrh . . ." We remember the wise men. They, too, knew this was a special child. According to tradition there were three wise men, but we don't know for sure how many there were. We do know, however, that they came from the East to worship him who was born to save the world.

Reader One: "Now when Jesus was born in Bethlehem of Judea in the days of Herod the king, behold, there came wise men from the east to Jerusalem, Saying, Where is he that is born King of the Jews? for we have seen his star in the east, and are come to worship him. When Herod the king had heard these things, he was troubled, and all Jerusalem with him. And when he had gathered all the

chief priests and scribes of the people together, he demanded of them where Christ should be born. And they
said unto him, In Bethlehem of Judea: for thus it is written
by the prophet, And thou Bethlehem, in the land of Juda,
art not the least among the princes of Juda: for out of thee
shall come a Governor, that shall rule my people Israel"
(Matt. 2:1–6).

Reader Two: "And when they were come into the house,
they saw the young child with Mary his mother, and fell
down, and worshipped him: and when they had opened
their treasures, they presented unto him gifts; gold, and
frankincense, and myrrh" (Matt. 2:11).

(Wise men enter and walk to Mary, Joseph and the babe)

Song: We Three Kings of Orient Are *(All boys)*

>We three kings of Orient are,
>   Bearing gifts we traverse afar
>Field and fountain, moor and mountain,
>   Following yonder star.
>
>Refrain:
>O star of wonder, star of night,
>   Star with royal beauty bright,
>Westward leading, still proceeding,
>   Guide us to thy perfect light.
>
>Born a king on Bethlehem's plain,
>   Gold I bring to crown him again,
>King forever, ceasing never
>   Over us all to reign.
>
>Frankincense to offer have I,
>   Incense owns a deity nigh;
>Prayer and praising, all men raising,
>   Worship him, God on high.
>
>Myrrh is mine; its bitter perfume
>   Breathes a life of gathering gloom:

Sorrowing, sighing, bleeding, dying,
   Sealed in the stone-cold tomb.

Glorious now behold him arise,
   King and God and Sacrifice;
Alleluia, alleluia!
   Sounds through the earth and skies.
                    John H. Hopkins, Jr

Narrator: When Jesus was eight days old, Mary and Joseph brought him to the temple at Jerusalem to be circumcised. Old Simeon saw Jesus and knew that he was the child God had promised to send as the Savior. He held Jesus in his arms and said, "Lord, now lettest thou thy servant depart in peace, according to thy word: For mine eyes have seen thy salvation, which thou hast prepared before the face of all people; A light to lighten the Gentiles, and the glory of thy people Israel" (Luke 2:29–32).

As more and more Christmas seasons come and go, it's easy to lose the excitement and wonder which we felt the first time we heard the story of Jesus' birth. In all the hustle of buying and receiving gifts, may we never forget the greatest Gift of all: Jesus Christ who gave himself for us. He has called us to be his people; he has purchased us with his blood. We belong to him and nothing can separate us from his love. That's why the Christmas story is told from generation to generation. It's an old, old story, yet always new!

Song: For God So Loved the World *(All children)*

For God so loved the world he gave his only Son
   To die on Calvary's tree from sin to set me free.
Some day he's coming back—
   What glory that will be!
Wonderful his love to me.

Narrator: We pray that our celebration today may have helped you to understand more fully the real meaning of Christmas. A blessed Christmas to all!

Song: O Jesus, We Adore Thee *(Audience)*

> O Jesus, we adore thee,
>   Upon the cross, our King!
> We bow our hearts before thee,
>   Thy gracious name we sing.
> That name hath brought salvation,
>   That name in life our stay,
> Our peace, our consolation,
>   When life shall fade away.
>
> O glorious King, we bless thee,
>   No longer pass thee by;
> O Jesus, we confess thee
>   The Son enthroned on high.
> Lord, grant to us remission;
>   Life through thy death restore;
> Yea, grant us the fruition
>   Of life for evermore.
>   Arthur T. Russell

Written by Arlene Hoeksema for the Bethel Christian Reformed Church School program December, 1979.

10

The Puppets Celebrate Christmas

Cast

Narrator

Puppets—

Angela

Bernard

Gramps

Lion

Ovie

(On stage the choir is seated. Spotlights on the Cross and the puppet stage. Bernard, Gramps and Angela are on the puppet stage.)

Bernard: Christmas season is here! I can't wait until Christmas morning when I get up and run to the tree. There'll be all kinds of presents just for me. Yippee!

Angela: That's right! I made a big list of the gifts that I want this year. I sure hope that I get all of them.

Bernard: This is my favorite time of year. I just love Christmas!

Gramps: *(He has been shaking his head as Bernard and Angela talk.)* Don't you two think there's more to Christmas than gifts? Gifts have certainly become an important

150

part of Christmas to us, but there are some things far more important.

Angela: Gramps, you're right, but it's so exciting thinking about all the presents we may get. It's easy to forget that the real reason we celebrate is that Jesus was born and came to earth on Christmas Day.

(The puppets disappear and there is complete silence in the sanctuary for a short period of time.)

Song: It Came Upon the Midnight Clear *(Choir)*

> It came upon the midnight clear,
>   That glorious song of old,
> From angels bending near the earth
>   To touch their harps of gold:
> "Peace on the earth, goodwill to men,
>   From heaven's all-gracious King!"
> The world in solemn stillness lay
>   To hear the angels sing.
>
> Still through the cloven skies they come,
>   With peaceful wings unfurled;
> And still their heavenly music floats
>   O'er all the weary world;
> Above its sad and lowly plains
>   They bend on hovering wing;
> And ever o'er its Babel sounds.
>   The blessed angels sing.
>
> And ye, beneath life's crushing load,
>   Whose forms are bending low,
> Who toil along the climbing way
>   With painful steps and slow,
> Look now! for glad and golden hours
>   Come swiftly on the wing;
> O rest beside the weary road,
>   And hear the angels sing!
>
>   E. H. Sears

(Puppets' stage lights dim to blackout.)

Narrator: The Christmas story is nearly two thousand years old. Each year as December twenty-fifth approaches the story is repeated time and time again. Most of us learn the story when we are children and as we grow up we hear the story anew each year.

Song: Silent Night, Holy Night *(Choir)*

> Silent night, holy night,
>   All is calm, all is bright
> Round yon virgin mother and child.
>   Holy infant so tender and mild,
> Sleep in heavenly peace,
> Sleep in heavenly peace.
>
> Silent night, holy night,
>   Shepherds quake at the sight,
> Glories stream from heaven afar,
>   Heavenly hosts sing alleluia;
> Christ, the Savior, is born!
> Christ, the Savior, is born!
>
> Silent night, holy night,
>   Son of God, love's pure light
> Radiant beams from thy holy face,
>   With the dawn of redeeming grace,
> Jesus, Lord, at thy birth,
> Jesus, Lord, at thy birth.
>
>   Joseph Mohr

Narrator: Even though the story is so familiar, it is one that we never tire of hearing. For the Christmas story is one of *love*. The Son of God came to earth as a baby. As he grew up and lived among people he realized that his basic purpose in coming was to give his life on the cross for our sins.

(Puppet stage lights come on.)

Song: Love Came Down at Christmas *(Choir)*

> Love came down at Christmas,
>   Love all lovely, Love divine;
> Love was born at Christmas,
>   Star and angels gave the sign.
>
> Worship we the Godhead,
>   Love incarnate, Love divine;
> Worship we our Jesus;
>   But wherewith for sacred sign?
>
> Love shall be our token,
>   Love be yours and love be mine,
> Love to God and all men,
>   Love for plea and gift and sign.
>   Christina Rossetti

(As the song ends, the Lion and Ovie appear.)

Lion: Ho, Ho, Ho! Merry Christmas everybody!

Ovie: Who in the world do you think you are?

Lion: I'm Santa Claus. Don't I look like him?

Ovie: Well, I don't see any whiskers.

(Angela appears.)

Lion: Who needs whiskers? I love people! I love children! I love everybody! So I should be able to be Santa Claus if I want to be. Ho, Ho, Ho! Merry Christmas everybody!

Angela: Well, Mr. Lion, I'm a Christian and I love everybody too. But the reason we celebrate Christmas is that Jesus came to earth nearly two thousand years ago. We can make people much happier than Santa Claus can because we can introduce them to Jesus and he can live in their hearts. When Jesus lives in a person's heart, he helps that person love everybody. That's why Christmas is so important today. This world needs the love that Christians have in their hearts.

(Puppets disappear.)

Song: The Great God of Heaven *(Choir)*

> The great God of heaven is come down to earth,
> His mother a virgin, and sinless his birth;
> The Father eternal his Father alone:
> He sleeps in the manger; he reigns on the throne:
>
> Refrain:
> Then let us adore him, and praise his great love:
> To save us poor sinners he came from above.
>
> A babe on the breast of a maiden he lies,
> Yet sits with the Father on high in the skies;
> Before him their faces the seraphim hide,
> While Joseph stands waiting, unscared, by his side:
>
> Lo! here is Emmanuel, here is the child,
> The son that was promised to Mary so mild;
> Whose power and dominion shall ever increase,
> The Prince that shall rule o'er a kingdom of peace:
>
> The wonderful counselor, boundless in might,
> The Father's own image, the beam of his light;
> Behold him now wearing the likeness of man,
> Weak, helpless, and speechless, in measure a span:
>
> O wonder of wonders, which none can unfold:
> The ancient of days is an hour or two old;
> The maker of all things is made of the earth,
> Man is worshiped by angels, and God comes to birth:
>
> The Word in the bliss of the Godhead remains,
> Yet in flesh comes to suffer the keenest of pains;
> He is that he was, and for ever shall be,
> But becomes that he was not, for you and for me.
>
> > H. R. Bramley

(As song ends, Bernard, Gramps, and Ovie appear.)

Gramps: Say, Ovie, do you know what a financial genius is?

Ovie: No, Gramps. What's a financial genius?

Gramps: A financial genius is a person who can figure out how to pay all of the family's Christmas debts in January. *(pause)* Now a more serious question. Bernard, what's it like in the department stores right now?

Bernard: I'll tell you. I couldn't believe it! I went to a store to buy a present for my mother and there was shoving and pushing and some people were saying bad words.

Ovie: Isn't that the truth? I was at the store today and was going to buy one of those new computerized football games for my brother. I reached for one on the shelf and it was the last one. A man grabbed my wrist and pushed me away and said, "That's mine. I want to buy that game."

Gramps: Christmas is supposed to be a time of love and peace. But in stores and other places some people fight with other people. We can see the same attitude between countries as they fight with each other. One of the reasons Jesus came to earth was to bring peace and he still wants us to live in peace today.

(Puppets disappear.)

Song: O God, to Thine Anointed King *(Choir)*

> O God, to thine anointed King
> Give truth and righteousness;
> Thy people he will justly judge
> And give the poor redress.
> Then every fruitful mountainside
> Shall yield its rich increase,
> And righteousness in all the land
> Shall bear the fruit of peace.

Like rain upon the new-mown grass,
  That falls refreshingly,
Like gentle showers that cheer the earth,
  So shall his coming be.
The righteous in his glorious day
  Shall flourish and increase;
The earth, until the moon shall fade,
  Shall have abundant peace.

G. T. Alexis

(As choir finishes song, puppet stage lights dim to blackout.)

Narrator: Because mankind as a whole has not accepted the message of Christ, there is no real peace on earth. However, when you and I become Christians and take Christ into our hearts, we can have that peace which he promised in our hearts and lives. It is that peace which will sustain and guide us through the many trials, temptations, problems, and failures which we experience as human beings. That peace can fill us because of the excitement, joy, and happiness that occurred on Christmas Day when Jesus Christ was born.

(Puppet stage lights come up.)

Solo: Coventry Carol

(All five puppets appear.)

Angela: Hey, I've got an idea.

Bernard: What's your idea, Angela?

Angela: Let's put on a Christmas skit.

Ovie: Okay, but what should we do?

Angela: Well, let's have Mary and Joseph, the three wise men, and the shepherds.

Lion: What can I be?

Angela: Well, I'll be Mary.

Ovie: I'll be Joseph.

Gramps: Well, that leaves Bernard, Lion, and me to be the wise men. *(He looks in the direction of the choir.)* Maybe we can put on this skit while the choir sings.

Song: Christians, Awake, Salute the Happy Morn *(Choir)*

> Christians, awake, salute the happy morn,
> Whereon the Savior of the world was born;
> Rise to adore the mystery of love,
> Which hosts of angels chanted from above;
> With them the joyful tidings first begun
> Of God incarnate and the virgin's son:
>
> Then to the watchful shepherds it was told,
> Who heard the angelic herald's voice, "Behold,
> I bring good tidings of a Savior's birth
> To you and all the nations upon earth;
> This day hath God fulfilled his promised word,
> This day is born a Savior, Christ the Lord."
>
> He spake; and straightway the celestial choir
> In hymns of joy, unknown before, conspire.
> The praises of redeeming love they sang,
> And heaven's whole orb with Alleluias rang:
> God's highest glory was their anthem still,
> Peace upon earth, and mutual goodwill.
>
> To Bethlehem straight the enlightened shepherds ran,
> To see the wonder God had wrought for man,
> And found, with Joseph and the blessed maid,
> Her son, the Savior, in a manger laid;
> Amazed the wondrous story they proclaim,
> The first apostles of his infant fame.
>
> Like Mary let us ponder in our mind
> God's wondrous love in saving lost mankind;
> Trace we the babe, who hath retrieved our loss,

From his poor manger to his bitter cross;
Then may we hope, angelic throngs among,
To sing, redeemed, a glad triumphal song.

John Byrom

(As the choir completes the song, puppet stage lights dim to blackout.)

Narrator: Christmas is a time when everybody likes to join in the festivities. So at this time we would like to have you, the audience, join with us in singing two of the old-time favorite Christmas songs.

(Sanctuary lights and stage lights come on full.)

Songs: O Come, All Ye Faithful *(Audience)*

O come, all ye faithful, joyful and triumphant,
    O come ye, O come ye to Bethlehem;
Come and behold him, born the King of angels;

Refrain:
O come, let us adore him,
O come, let us adore him,
O come, let us adore him,
Christ, the Lord!

Sing, choirs of angels, sing in exultation,
    Sing, all ye citizens of heaven above!
Glory to God, all glory in the highest;

Yea, Lord, we greet thee, born this happy morning,
    Jesus, to thee be all glory given;
Word of the Father, now in flesh appearing;

John F. Wade
Tr. Frederick Oakeley

O Little Town of Bethlehem

O little town of Bethlehem,
    How still we see thee lie!

Above thy deep and dreamless sleep
　　The silent stars go by;
Yet in thy dark streets shineth
　　The everlasting Light;
The hopes and fears of all the years
　　Are met in thee tonight.

For Christ is born of Mary,
　　And gathered all above,
While mortals sleep, the angels keep
　　Their watch of wondering love.
O morning stars, together
　　Proclaim the holy birth!
And praises sing to God the King,
　　And peace to men on earth.

O holy Child of Bethlehem!
　　Descend to us, we pray;
Cast out our sin and enter in;
　　Be born in us today.
We hear the Christmas angels
　　The great glad tidings tell;
O come to us, abide with us,
　　Our Lord Emmanuel!
　　　　　　　　　　Phillips Brooks

Narrator: We've talked tonight about the love and the peace that Christ brought into the world when he was born. We've also heard songs about Christ's birth on Christmas Day. The Bible tells us that the shepherds and the angels also rejoiced at the birth of Jesus.

Song: Angels We Have Heard on High *(Choir)*

Angels we have heard on high
　　Sweetly singing o'er the plains,
And the mountains in reply
　　Echo back their joyous strains.

Refrain:
Gloria in excelsis Deo,
Gloria in excelsis Deo.

Shepherds, why this jubilee?
  Why your joyous strains prolong?
Say what may the tidings be,
  Which inspire your heavenly song.

Come to Bethlehem and see
  Him whose birth the angels sing;
Come, adore on bended knee,
  Christ, the Lord, the newborn King.
                Traditional French Carol

(Five puppets appear.)

Bernard: I sure wouldn't want to have been a shepherd guarding sheep.

Angela: Why not?

Bernard: Because I would have been scared! The shepherds had to protect their sheep and guard them from wolves and all kinds of wild animals like *lions*!

Lion: What do you mean—*lions*? I'm a lion and I wouldn't hurt anybody.

Ovie: That's just because you don't know any better.

Lion: You're not being very nice to me. I'm going to get you if you don't stop that!

Gramps: Now, now, children, settle down. We came here tonight to help the choir with their program and we don't want to spoil things now.

Lion: Okay, okay! But tell them to quit picking on me.

Gramps: They were just teasing you, but they won't do it anymore.

Angela: Tell us, Gramps, when did God decide to send Jesus to earth? Did he decide it a long, long time ago?

Gramps: God already promised Adam and Eve that he

would send a Savior to earth. The Old Testament prophets
all told of his coming. Isaiah especially told many details
about Jesus' coming.

(Puppets disappear.)

Song: Lo, How a Rose E'er Blooming *(Choir)*

> Lo, how a Rose e'er blooming
>   From tender stem hath sprung!
> Of Jesse's lineage coming
>   As men of old have sung.
> It came a floweret bright,
>   Amid the cold of winter,
> When half spent was the night.
>
> Isaiah 'twas foretold it,
>   The Rose I have in mind,
> With Mary we behold it,
>   The Virgin Mother kind.
> To show God's love aright,
>   She bore to men a Savior,
> When half spent was the night.
>   15th Century German
>   Tr. Theodore Baker

(Stage lights dim to blackout.)

Narrator: As we said earlier in the program, Jesus came to
earth knowing that his mission was to die on the cross for
your sins and my sins. That demanded real love. So Christmas is a time of happiness; it is a time of joy; it is a time of
celebration. We can do nothing but thank God for sending
his precious gift to earth on Christmas Day.

(Puppet stage lights come on. Five puppets appear.)

Angela: Its good to hear the Christmas story again. I'm
going to really enjoy this Christmas season.

Bernard: I'm not going to get so upset when I go Christmas shopping and people push me around. I'm going to remember the message of Christ.

Lion: I'm glad that Christ came to earth for me. I'm going to try to not get so angry when people tease me from now on.

Gramps: It's easy for a person to play Santa Claus. A person just has to buy a beard and put a pillow under his shirt. But it's also easy to forget the real meaning of the Christmas celebration—Jesus' birth, life, and death. We must invite Jesus into our hearts and lives so that we can know the joy and peace of having our sins forgiven.

Ovie: Because Jesus loves us so much that he gave himself for our sins on the cross, we can share his love as Christians. Let us all thank and praise him for his wonderful gift of love as the choir sings a song of celebration.

(Puppets disappear.)

Song: Thou Didst Leave Thy Throne *(Choir)*

> Thou didst leave thy throne and thy kingly crown
> When thou camest to earth for me,
> But in Bethlehem's home there was found no room
> For thy holy nativity.
> O come to my heart, Lord Jesus;
> There is room in my heart for thee!
>
> Heaven's arches rang when the angels sang,
> Proclaiming thy royal degree,
> But in lowly birth didst thou come to earth,
> And in great humility.
> O come to my heart, Lord Jesus;
> There is room in my heart for thee!
>   Emily E. S. Elliott

Written by Jan and Virgil Leatherman for the Orchard View Church of God, Grand Rapids, Michigan. Given Christmas, 1979.

11

Christmas—Past and Present

Why Do We Have Christmas?

Narrator: Why must we have Christmas? To answer that important question we need to go back to the beginning of history when God created the world.

Songs: Who Made Ocean, Earth, and Sky? *(Primary children)*

> Who made ocean, earth, and sky?
> > God, our loving Father.
> Who made sun and moon on high?
> > God, our loving Father.
> Who made all the birds that fly?
> > God, our loving Father.
>
> Who made lakes and rivers blue?
> > God, our loving Father.
> Who made snow and rain and dew?
> > God, our loving Father.
> He made little children too,
> > God, our loving Father.
> > > Richard Compton

All Things Bright and Beautiful

> Each little flower that opens,
> > Each little bird that sings—
> He made their glowing colors,
> > He made their tiny wings.

Refrain:
All things bright and beautiful,
    All creatures great and small,
All things wise and wonderful—
    The Lord God made them all.

The purple-headed mountain,
    The river running by,
The sunset and the morning
    That brighten up the sky.

The cold wind in the winter,
    The pleasant summer sun,
The ripe fruits in the garden—
    He made them, every one.

He gave us eyes to see them
    And lips that we might tell
How great is God Almighty,
    Who has made all things well.
                    Cecil F. Alexander

Song: How Great Thou Art *(Audience)*

O Lord my God, when I in awesome wonder
    Consider all the works thy hands have made,
I see the stars, I hear the mighty thunder
    Thy power throughout the universe displayed.

Refrain:
Then sings my soul, my Savior God, to thee;
    How great thou art, how great thou art!
Then sings my soul, my Savior God, to thee:
    How great thou art, how great thou art!

When through the woods and forest glades I wander
    And hear the birds sing sweetly in the trees,
When I look down from lofty mountain grandeur
    And hear the brook and feel the gentle breeze.
                    Stuart K. Kine

Narrator: *(As the narrator tells the creation story, children enter each carrying a prop representing parts of God's creation, such as sun, stars, trees, vegetables, and animals. These are placed on an appropriate background.)*

At first the world was darkness and confusion. Then God said, "Let there be light." The light appeared and it was the first day. On the second day God separated the waters on the earth from those in the sky.

The next thing God did was to separate the dry land from the water on the earth. Then he covered the earth with grass, flowers, trees, plants and shrubs. He made all varieties of fruits and vegetables. God did that on the third day.

Then God made, on the fourth day, the big, bright sun to give light and heat to the earth, and the moon and stars to shine at night. But the earth was quiet—there were no living creatures. So God made fish of all kinds to swim in the waters and God made all kinds of birds to fly through the air. "And God said, Let the earth bring forth the living creature after his kind, cattle, and creeping thing, and beast of the earth after his kind: and it was so" (Gen. 1:24). He made the little kittens and the white bunnies, the big elephants and the strong lions. The fifth day kept God very busy.

Finally, on the sixth and last day of his creative work, God made a man. He made him from dust and breathed into him the breath of life and man became a living soul. He was greater than all other creatures; he could think and speak, and he could know God. God named him Adam. As Adam gave names to all the birds, fish, and other animals he saw that they were all in pairs—males and females. But Adam had no mate who was fit for him. Then God caused Adam to sleep and from one of his ribs made a woman whom Adam named Eve.

(Children remain on stage with props as the audience sings, "This Is My Father's World.")

Song: This Is My Father's World *(Audience)*

> This is my Father's world,
>   And to my listening ears
> All nature sings, and round me rings
>   The music of the spheres.
> This is my Father's world:
>   I rest me in the thought
> Of rocks and trees, of skies and seas;
>   His hand the wonders wrought.
>
> This is my Father's world,
>   The birds their carols raise,
> The morning light, the lily white,
>   Declare their Maker's praise.
> This is my Father's world:
>   He shines in all that's fair;
> In the rustling grass I hear him pass,
>   He speaks to me everywhere.
>
> This is my Father's world,
>   O let me ne'er forget
> That though the wrong seems oft so strong,
>   God is the ruler yet.
> This is my Father's world:
>   The battle is not done;
> Jesus, who died, shall be satisfied,
>   And heaven and earth be one.
>   Maltbie Davenport Babcock

Narrator: *(Three children representing Adam, Eve, and the serpent pantomime the story of how sin entered the world as the narrator relates it.)*
     God gave Adam and Eve the beautiful Garden of Eden as their first home. God told Adam to take care of the garden, of the trees, plants, flowers, and animals. God said, "Of every tree of the garden thou mayest freely eat: But of the tree of the knowledge of good and evil, thou shalt not eat of it: for in the day that thou eatest thereof thou shalt surely die" (Gen. 2:16, 17).

Satan listened to God give Adam this commandment. He hates God and wants people to worship him instead of obeying God. He went to the Garden of Eden in the form of a beautiful snake. He went to Eve and asked, "Did God say you could not eat from every tree of the garden?"

Eve answered, "We may eat the fruit of the trees in this garden, except that of the middle tree. If we do, we shall surely die."

"You will not die," Satan sneered. "God knows that if you eat from that tree you will be just as wise as he is. That is why God doesn't want you to eat from that tree." Then Satan showed Eve how beautiful the tree was and how delicious the fruit looked.

When Eve saw the good fruit, and thought she might become wise like God, she took some and ate it. Then she gave some to Adam and he ate it too.

Adam and Eve's disobedience brought sin and death into the world just as God had said it would. All those born from Adam and Eve, down through all generations, are sinners and must face the punishment of death. However, God loved Adam and Eve just as he loves his people today. He gave them a wonderful promise: He said that someday he would send his own Son, Jesus Christ, to be the Savior of the world and to destroy Satan and all his followers.

Song: O Come, O Come, Emmanuel *(Audience)*

> O come, O come, Emmanuel,
>   And ransom captive Israel,
> That mourns in lonely exile here
>   Until the Son of God appear.
>
> Refrain:
> Rejoice! Rejoice!
>   Emmanuel
> Shall come to thee,
>   O Israel.

O come, thou branch of Jesse's stem,
   Unto thine own, and rescue them!
From depths of hell thy people save,
   And give them victory o'er the grave.

O come, thou Bright and Morning Star,
   And bring us comfort from afar!
Dispel the shadows of the night,
   And turn our darkness into light.

                    Anonymous Latin Hymn
                    Tr. John Mason Neal

What Is Christmas?

Narrator: The once perfect world was now polluted by sin. Man carried a heavy burden of guilt. The world needed a Savior. God provided that Savior in his own Son, the Lord Jesus.

Fourth Graders: *(As the children recite Luke 2:1–20, pictures drawn by second graders are flashed on the screen at appropriate times. Soft background music is played on the organ.)*

And it came to pass in those days, that there went out a decree from Caesar Augustus, that all the world should be taxed. (And this taxing was first made when Cyrenius was governor of Syria.) And all went to be taxed, everyone into his own city. And Joseph also went up from Galilee, out of the city of Nazareth, into Judea, unto the city of David, which is called Bethlehem; (because he was of the house and lineage of David:) To be taxed with Mary his espoused wife, being great with child. And so it was, that, while they were there, the days were accomplished that she should be delivered. And she brought forth her firstborn son, and wrapped him in swaddling clothes, and laid him in a manger; because there was no room for them in the inn. And there were in the same country shepherds abiding in the field, keeping watch over their flock by night. And, lo, the angel of the Lord came upon them, and the glory of the Lord shone round about them: and they were sore afraid. And the angel said unto them, Fear not: for, behold, I bring you tidings of great joy, which shall be to all people. For unto you is born this day in the city of David a Saviour, which is Christ the Lord. And this shall be a sign unto you; Ye shall find the babe wrapped in swaddling clothes, lying in a manger. And suddenly there was with the angel a multitude of the heavenly host praising God, and saying, Glory to God in the highest, and on earth peace, good will toward men. And it came to pass, as the angels were gone away from them into heaven, the shepherds said one to another, Let us now go even unto Bethlehem, and see this thing which is come to pass, which the Lord hath made known unto us. And they came with haste, and found Mary, and Joseph, and the babe lying in a manger. And when they had seen it, they made known abroad the saying which was told them concerning this child. And all they that heard it wondered at those things which were told them by the shepherds. But Mary kept all these things, and pondered them in her heart.

Narrator: *(The story of the wise men is illustrated by pictures drawn by the third graders.)*

Now when Jesus was born in Bethlehem of Judea in the days of Herod the king, behold, there came wise men from the east to Jerusalem, Saying, Where is he that is born King of the Jews? for we have seen his star in the east, and are come to worship him. When Herod the king had heard these things, he was troubled, and all Jerusalem with him. And when he had gathered all the chief priests and scribes of the people together, he demanded of them where Christ should be born. And they said unto him, In Bethlehem of Judea: for thus it is written by the prophet, And thou Bethlehem, in the land of Juda, art not the least among the princes of Juda: for out of thee shall come a Governor, that shall rule my people Israel. Then Herod, when he had privily called the wise men, enquired of them diligently what time the star appeared. And he sent them to Bethlehem, and said, Go and search diligently for the young child; and when ye have found him, bring me word again, that I may come and worship him also. When they had heard the king, they departed; and, lo, the star, which they saw in the east, went before them, till it came and stood over where the young child was. When they saw the star, they rejoiced with exceeding great joy. And when they were come into the house, they saw the young child with Mary his mother, and fell down, and worshipped him: and when they had opened their treasures, they presented unto him gifts; gold, and frankincense, and myrrh. (Matthew 2:1–11)

Song: Away In a Manger *(Primary children)*

> Away in a manger, no crib for his bed,
>   The little Lord Jesus lay down his sweet head;
> The stars in the heavens looked down where he lay,
>   The little Lord Jesus asleep in the hay.
>
> The cattle are lowing, the baby awakes,
>   But little Lord Jesus, no crying he makes;
> I love thee, Lord Jesus, look down from the sky,
>   And stay by my cradle till morning is nigh.
>
> Be near me, Lord Jesus! I ask thee to stay
>   Close by me forever, and love me, I pray.
> Bless all the dear children in thy tender care,
>   And take us to heaven to live with thee there.
>
> Anonymous

Song: Hark! the Herald Angels Sing *(Audience)*

> Hark! the herald angels sing,
>   "Glory to the newborn King;
> Peace on earth, and mercy mild,
>   God and sinners reconciled!"
> Joyful, all ye nations, rise,

Join the triumph of the skies;
With the angelic host proclaim,
   "Christ is born in Bethlehem."

Refrain:
   Hark! the herald angels sing,
   "Glory to the newborn King!"

Christ, by highest heaven adored;
   Christ, the everlasting Lord!
Late in time behold him come,
   Offspring of the virgin's womb.
Veiled in flesh the Godhead see;
   Hail the incarnate deity,
Pleased as man with men to dwell,
   Jesus, our Emmanuel.

Hail the heavenborn Prince of peace!
   Hail the Sun of righteousness!
Light and life to all he brings,
   Risen with healing in his wings,
Mild he lays his glory by,
   Born that man no more may die,
Born to raise the sons of earth,
   Born to give them second birth.
                                    Charles Wesley

Youth Choir: On this Day Earth Shall Ring
               On Christmas Night
               (*or similar carols*)

What Is Our Response to Christmas?

Narrator: (*The following presentation was illustrated with
   slides showing the ministry of the church as it reaches out
   from the local congregation to the ends of the earth.*)
      God sent his Son to take upon himself the burden of our
sin. We are set free to serve him. His love abides in us and
is expressed in our everyday lives. Christ has commanded
us to love God above all and our neighbors as ourselves.

There are many ways to show our love for God and for one another. We gather in churches to praise God, to listen to his Word, and to pray for his people everywhere. Jesus promised, "Where two or three are gathered together in my name there am I in the midst of them" (Matt. 18:20).

Christians all around the world say, "I was glad when they said unto me, Let us go into the house of the Lord." God speaks to us through our pastor and church leaders. We hear God's message and respond in prayer, praise and giving of gifts. Some of our gifts are used to support missionaries, some are used to translate and distribute Bibles and Christian literature. We help those who train people to make good use of their land and water. We also use our money to help our own church family grow and become strong in the Lord.

Loving our neighbors as ourselves is expressed in many ways: a letter or card sent to cheer or comfort someone is one way to show concern for others. In Galatians 6:2 we read, "Bear ye one another's burdens, and so fulfil the law of Christ." Sometimes a kind word, a gesture of understanding, or a listening ear gives hope and courage to a struggling person. Our love and concern for others can also be expressed with financial gifts.

When Jesus comes again he will say to his faithful children,

> For I was an hungred, and ye gave me meat: I was thirsty, and ye gave me drink: I was a stranger, and ye took me in: Naked, and ye clothed me: I was sick, and ye visited me: I was in prison, and ye came unto me. Then shall the righteous answer him, saying, Lord, when saw we thee an hungred, and fed thee? or thirsty, and gave thee to drink? When saw we thee a stranger, and took thee in? or naked, and clothed thee? Or when saw we thee sick, or in prison, and came unto thee? And the King shall answer and say unto them, Verily I say unto you, Inasmuch as ye have done it unto one of the least of these my brethren, ye have done it unto me. (Matt. 25:35–40)

Only a few evidences of our love for God and our neighbors have been shown tonight. May this Christmas season remind us again of God's great love to us and help us find new ways to share that gift of love with others.

Song: What Can I Give Him *(Third and fourth graders)*

> What can I give him,
>   Poor as I am?
> If I were a shepherd,
>   I would bring a lamb;
> If I were a wise man,
>   I would do my part;
> Yet what I can I give him—
>   Give my heart.
>   Christina G. Rossetti

Song: How Great Thou Art *(Audience)*

O Lord my God, when I in awesome wonder
    Consider all the works thy hands have made,
I see the stars, I hear the mighty thunder
    Thy power throughout the universe displayed.

Refrain:
Then sings my soul, my Savior God, to thee;
    How great thou art, how great thou art!
Then sings my soul, my Savior God, to thee:
    How great thou art, how great thou art!

When through the woods and forest glades I wander
    And hear the birds sing sweetly in the trees,
When I look down from lofty mountain grandeur
    And hear the brook and feel the gentle breeze.
                                    Stuart K. Kine

This program was presented at the First Christian Reformed Church, Allendale (Michigan), Christmas, 1977. It was coordinated by Janice Sall. The young people made the props for Part 1; the second- and third-grade children drew pictures which were made into slides illustrating Part 2 of the program. Its presentation involved the entire congregation.

12

Wonderful Christmas

Processional: Wonderful Words of Life

Sing them over again to me, wonderful words of life;
Let me more of their beauty see, wonderful words of life.
Words of life and beauty, teach me faith and duty:
   Beautiful words, wonderful words, wonderful words of
     life.
   Beautiful words, wonderful words, wonderful words of
     life.

Christ, the blessed one gives to all wonderful words of life;
Listen well to the loving call, wonderful words of life.
All the wondrous story, showing us His glory:
   Beautiful words, wonderful words, wonderful words of
     life.
   Beautiful words, wonderful words, wonderful words of
     life.

Sweetly echo the gospel call, wonderful words of life;
Offer pardon and peace to all, wonderful words of life.
Jesus, only Savior, sanctify forever:
   Beautiful words, wonderful words, wonderful words of
     life.
   Beautiful words, wonderful words, wonderful words of
     life.

Philip P. Bliss

Welcome: We are happy to have you join us in a Christmas
celebration. We want you to consider with us a beautiful
word found in the Bible several times. *(Points to the word*

WONDERFUL which is suspended from the ceiling over the stage.)

Prayer: Father in heaven, we remember Christ's wonderful birth tonight. We remember that thy wonderful love sent Jesus as a babe to the manger of Bethlehem. We thank thee for sending him not only to Bethlehem, but also to Calvary to die for our sins. Just as the star guided the shepherds and the wise men to Bethlehem, may we, thy children, guide this audience to our Savior. In Jesus name we pray. Amen.

Narrator: How frequently we use the word *wonderful* in our daily conversation! We tell our friends we have wonderful children. We boast of wonderful food, a wonderful cook, and wonderful holidays. We enjoy wonderful health, and music and friends. We speak of a wonderful joy and wonderful weather. But did you know that the word *wonderful* is the title given to our Lord? Tonight we are going to consider the wonderfuls of Christmas.

(Ten children come forward, in pairs, carrying banners which they raise one at a time and together read the words on the signs:)

> WONDERFUL PROMISE
>
> WONDERFUL BIRTH
>
> WONDERFUL STAR
>
> WONDERFUL GIFT
>
> WONDERFUL SAVIOR

Narrator: *(pointing to the banners)* These are the wonderfuls which we will share tonight.

Part 1: Promises

(Two children holding the banner WONDERFUL PROMISES step forward.)

First Child: Promises, promises, promises! Sometimes it seems that all we get are promises and nothing more!

Second Child: God made a promise to us centuries ago through the prophet Isaiah. God kept his promise, and that is the reason for our celebration tonight.

Both Children: "For unto us a child is born, unto us a son is given: and the government shall be upon his shoulder: and his name shall be called Wonderful, Counselor, the mighty God, the everlasting Father, the Prince of Peace."

Song: Standing on the Promises *(Audience)*

Standing on the promises of Christ my King,
    Through eternal ages let his praises ring!
Glory in the highest I will shout and sing—
    Standing on the promises of God,
    Standing on the promises of God!

Standing on the promises that cannot fail
    When the howling storms of doubt and fear assail;
By the living word of God I shall prevail—
    Standing on the promises of God,
    Standing on the promises of God!

                                        R. Kelso Carter

Part 2: Birth

(Two children holding the banner WONDERFUL BIRTH step forward.)

First Child: When the time came for Jesus to be born, God sent his angel, Gabriel, to Nazareth to tell Mary that she would become the mother of this Wonderful Child.

Second Child: Mary was afraid when she saw Gabriel but he said to her, "Fear not, Mary: for thou hast found favour with God. And, behold, thou shalt conceive in thy womb, and bring forth a son, and shalt call his name JESUS. He

shall be great, and shall be called the Son of the Highest:
and the Lord God shall give unto him the throne of his
father David: and he shall reign over the house of Jacob for
ever; and of his kingdom there shall be no end."

Narrator: But Jesus was not born in Nazareth. Our Wonderful God who controls all things, arranged world affairs
in such a way that Jesus would be born in Bethlehem as the
prophet Micah foretold.

> "And it came to pass in those days, that there went out a
> decree from Caesar Augustus, that all the world should be
> taxed. . . . And all went to be taxed, every one to his own
> city. And Joseph also went up from Galilee, out of the city
> of Nazareth, into Judea, unto the city of David, which is
> called Bethlehem . . . to be taxed with Mary his espoused
> wife, being great with child. And so it was, that, while they
> were there, the days were accomplished that she should be
> delivered. And she brought forth her firstborn son, and
> wrapped him in swaddling clothes, and laid him in a man-
> ger; because there was no room for them in the inn."

Song: O Little Town of Bethlehem *(Audience)*

O little town of Bethlehem, how still we see thee lie!
Above thy deep and dreamless sleep the silent stars go by.
Yet in thy dark streets shineth the everlasting Light;
The hopes and fears of all the years are met in thee tonight.

For Christ is born of Mary, and gathered all above,
While mortals sleep, the angels keep their watch of
    wond'ring love.
O morning stars, together proclaim the holy birth,
And praises sing to God the King, and peace to men on
    earth.

How silently, how silently the wondrous gift is giv'n!
So God imparts to human hearts the blessings of his
    heav'n.

No ear may hear his coming, but in this world of sin,
Where meek souls will receive him still, the dear Christ
  enters in.

Phillips Brooks

Part 3: Star

(Two children holding the banner WONDERFUL STAR step forward.)

First Child: What a wonderful thing that God chose a star to guide the Wise Men to Bethlehem! Jesus himself is the Star whose coming was foretold by Balaam, the prophet.

Second Child: Balaam said, "I shall see him, but not now: I shall behold him, but not nigh: there shall come a Star out of Jacob, and a Sceptre shall rise out of Israel, and shall smite the corners of Moab, and destroy all the children of Sheth." (Num. 24:17)

First Child: In the last book of the Bible, in his final message to the churches, Jesus called himself the bright and morning star.

Both Children: "I Jesus have sent mine angel to testify unto you these things in the churches. I am the root and the offspring of David, and the bright and morning star."

Narrator: We no longer need a star to guide us to Jesus. We have God's own Word. "And the Word was made flesh, and dwelt among us, (and we beheld his glory, the glory as of the only begotten of the Father,) full of grace and truth." Peter tells us, "We have also a more sure word of prophecy; whereunto ye do well that ye take heed, as unto a light that shineth in a dark place, until the day dawn, and the day star arise in your hearts."

Solo: There's a Song in the Air

  There's a song in the air!
  There's a star in the sky!

There's a mother's deep prayer
   And a baby's low cry!
And the star rains its fire while the beautiful sing,
   For the manger of Bethlehem cradles a King!

There's a tumult of joy
   O'er the wonderful birth,
For the virgin's sweet boy
   Is the Lord of the earth.
And the star rains its fire while the beautiful sing,
   For the manger of Bethlehem cradles a King!

We rejoice in the light,
   And we echo the song
That comes down through the night
   From the heavenly throng.
Ay! we shout to the wonderful message they bring,
   For the manger of Bethlehem cradles a King!

Josiah G. Holland

Part 4: Gift

*(Two children holding the banner WONDERFUL GIFT
step forward.)*

Narrator: Gift giving is a big part of our Christmas celebration. We sometimes worry about what we are going to get. We also worry that we might forget to buy a gift for someone, or that the persons for whom we do buy might not like our gifts. All these worries and frustrations over gift giving take away from the real meaning of the wonderful Gift.

First Child: "For God so loved the world, that he gave his only begotten Son, that whosoever believeth in him should not perish, but have everlasting life."

Second Child: "For the wages of sin is death; but the gift of God is eternal life through Jesus Christ our Lord."

Both Children: "Thanks be to God for His unspeakable gift!"

Recitation: Incarnate Love

> Love came down at Christmas,
>   Love all lovely, Love divine;
> Love was born at Christmas,
>   Star and angels gave the sign.
>
> Worship we the Godhead,
>   Love incarnate, Love divine;
> Worship we our Jesus;
>   But wherewith for sacred sign?
>
> Love shall be our token,
>   Love be yours and love be mine,
> Love to God and all men,
>   Love for plea and gift and sign.
>   Christina M. Rossetti

Songs: In the Bleak Midwinter *(Youth Choir)*

> In the bleak midwinter, frosty wind made moan,
> Earth stood hard as iron, water like a stone;
> Snow had fallen, snow on snow, snow on snow,
> In the bleak midwinter, long ago.
>
> Our God, heaven cannot hold him, nor earth sustain;
> Heaven and earth shall flee away when he comes to reign.
> In the bleak midwinter a stableplace sufficed
> The Lord God Almighty, Jesus Christ.
>
> Angels and archangels may have gathered there,
> Churubim and seraphim thronged the air;
> But only his mother, in her maiden bliss,
> Worshiped her beloved with a kiss.
>
> What can I give him, poor as I am?
> If I were a shepherd, I would bring a lamb;
> If I were a wise man, I would do my part;
> Yet what I can I give him—give my heart.
>   Christina Rossetti

I Gave My Life for Thee *(Audience)*

> I gave my life for thee,
>   My precious blood I shed;
> That thou might'st ransomed be,
>   And quickened from the dead;
> I gave, I gave my life for thee,
>   What hast thou done for me?
>
> My Father's house of light,
>   My glory circled throne
> I left for earthly night,
>   For wand'rings sad and lone;
> I left, I left it all for thee,
>   Hast thou left aught for me?
>
> I suffered much for thee,
>   More than thy tongue can tell,
> Of bitt'rest agony,
>   To rescue thee from hell;
> I've borne, I've borne it all for thee,
>   What hast thou borne for me?
>
> And I have brought to thee,
>   Down from my home above,
> Salvation full and free,
>   My pardon and my love;
> I bring, I bring rich gifts to thee,
>   What hast thou brought to me?
>   Frances R. Havergal

Narrator: God has blessed our nation with the riches of the earth. We hear from missionaries around the world and in parts of our own country of the physical needs of the people with whom they work. Now we are going to give you an opportunity to show your gratitude to God for his unspeakable gift by giving to help others who are not blessed as we are.

Offertory: Appropriate piano or organ solo.

Part 5: Savior

(Two children holding the banner WONDERFUL SAV-IOR step forward.)

Narrator: We often forget the real reason Jesus came into the world. We get so wrapped up in the baby Jesus, the star, the shepherds, the wise men, the total beauty of the Christmas pageantry that we forget that Jesus came into the world to die. Why did he come to die? He came so that you and I may live. Will you go with Jesus to the cross of Calvary and accept him as your Savior? Only then will you experience Christmas joy and peace. Only then will you truly have a wonderful Christmas.

Song: A Wonderful Savior Is Jesus My Lord *(Audience)*

> A wonderful Savior is Jesus my Lord,
>   A wonderful Savior to me;
> He hideth my soul in the cleft of the rock,
>   Where rivers of pleasure I see.
>
> Refrain:
> He hideth my soul in the cleft of the rock
>   That shadows a dry, thirsty land;
> He hideth my life in the depths of his love,
>   And covers me there with his hand,
>   And covers me there with his hand.
>
> A wonderful Savior is Jesus my Lord,
>   He taketh my burden away;
> He holdeth me up, and I shall not be moved;
>   He giveth me strength as my day.
>   Fanny J. Crosby

Speech Choir: A Christmas Hymn

(The choir is divided into two sections. The groups stand on opposite sides of the stage. One group asks the questions and the other gives the answers.)

Q: Tell me what is this innumerable throng
    Singing in the heavens a loud angelic song?

A: **These are they who come with swift and shining feet from
    round about the throne of God the Lord of Light to greet.**

Q: O, who are these that hasten beneath the starry sky,
    As if with joyful tidings that through the world shall fly?

A: **The faithful shepherds these, who greatly were afeared
    when, as they watched their flocks by night, the heavenly
    host appeared.**

Q: Who are these that follow across the hills of night
    A star that westward hurries along the fields of light?

A: **Three wise men from the east who myrrh and treasure
    bring to lay them at the feet of him, their Lord and Christ
    and King.**

Q: What babe new-born is this that in a manger cries?
    Near on her bed of pain his happy mother lies.

A: **O, see! the air is shaken with white and heavenly wings—
    This is the Lord of all the earth, This is the King of kings.**

Q: Tell me, how may I join in this holy feast
    With all the kneeling world, and I of all the least?

A: **Fear not, O faithful heart, but bring what most is meet;
    Bring love alone, true love alone, and lay it at his feet.**
                                                    Richard Watson Gilder

Narrator: "But now is Christ risen from the dead, and be-
    come the firstfruits of them that slept. For since by man
    came death, by man came also the resurrection of the
    dead. . . . Death is swallowed up in victory. O death,
    where is thy sting? O grave, where is thy victory? The
    sting of death is sin; and the strength of sin is the law. But

thanks be to God, which giveth us the victory through our Lord Jesus Christ." (1 Cor. 15:20, 21, 54b–57)

Songs: Now Let Every Tongue Adore Thee *(Children's choir)*

> Now let every tongue adore thee!
>   Let men with angels sing before thee!
> Let harps and cymbals now unite!
>   Heaven's gates with pearl are glorious,
> Where we partake through faith victorious,
>   With angels round thy throne of light.
> No mortal eye hath seen,
>   No mortal ear hath heard such wondrous things;
> Therefore with joy our song shall soar
>   In praise to God forevermore.
>
>   Philipp Nicolai
>   Tr. Paul English

Praise Him! Praise Him! *(Audience)*

> Praise him! praise him! Jesus, our blessed Redeemer!
>   Sing, O earth, his wonderful love proclaim!
> Hail him! hail him! highest archangels in glory;
>   Strength and honor give to his holy name!
> Like a shepherd, Jesus will guard his children,
>   In his arms he carries them all day long:
>
> Refrain:
> Praise him! praise him! tell of his excellent greatness;
> Praise him! praise him! ever in joyful song.
>
> Praise him! praise him! Jesus, our blessed Redeemer!
>   Heavenly portals loud with hosannas ring!
> Jesus, Savior, reigneth for ever and ever;
>   Crown him! crown him! Prophet, and Priest, and King!
> Christ is coming! over the world victorious,
>   Power and glory unto the Lord belong:

Prayer: We thank thee, Lord, for a wonderful Christmas celebration. We thank thee for the wonderful promise, birth, star, gift, and above all for our wonderful Savior. Amen.

Benediction: God bless and keep you on your way,
God give you a wonderful Christmas
And wonderful day.

Recessional: Wonderful Words of Life *(organ and piano)*

This program was adapted from one written by Elaine Bruxvoort for the Hope Christian Reformed Church of Stony Plain, Alberta, Canada, given Christmas, 1985.

PART THREE

Recitations and Exercises

13

The Twelve Days of Christmas

The following exercise was done by a class of high-school students. They sang a parody of "The Twelve Days of Christmas" as they brought their gifts forward. They planned in advance who would be the recipients of the gifts, and purchased them with their own money. All the participants remained front stage until every gift was brought forward. They designated certain members of the class to deliver the items to the family after the program as many of the things were perishable. Many youngsters can be involved in this project as they can double or triple the multiple items. Numerous variations of gifts can be used. Their twelve days included the following:

First day . . . . one juicy ham

Second day . . . . two Golden books

Third day . . . . three cans of fruit

Fourth day . . . . four children's toys

Fifth day . . . . five Christmas ornaments

Sixth day . . . . six cans of pop (soda)

Seventh day . . . . seven boxes of cracker-jacks

Eighth day . . . . eight lollipops

Ninth day . . . . nine candy canes

Tenth day . . . . ten pounds of potatoes

Eleventh day . . . . eleven oranges

Twelfth day . . . . twelve apples

Planned and supervised by Julia Vogel for a class at the Fifth Reformed Church of Grand Rapids, Michigan.

14

Christian Paradox

It is in loving—not in being loved,—
    The heart is blest;
It is in giving—not in seeking gifts,—
    We find our quest.

If thou art hungry, lacking heavenly food,—
    Give hope and cheer.
If thou art sad and wouldst be comforted,—
    Stay sorrow's tear.

Whatever be thy longing and thy need,—
    That do thou give;
So shall thy soul be fed, and thou indeed,
    Shalt truly live.

                    Author Unknown

15

Prayer on Christmas Eve

O wondrous night of star and song,
  O blessed Christmas night!
Lord, make me feel my whole life long
  Its loveliness and light!
So all the years my heart shall thrill
  Remembering angels on a hill,
And one lone star shall bless me still
  On every Christmas night!
                Nancy Byrd Turner

16

A Christmas Prayer

We open here our treasures and our gifts;
And some of it is gold,
And some is frankincense,
And some is myrrh;
For some has come from plenty,
Some from joy,
And some from deepest sorrow of the soul.
But thou, O God dost know the gift is love,
Our pledge of peace, our promise of good-will.
Accept the gift and all the life we bring.

Herbert H. Hines

17

Our Christmas Prayer

God grant you peace at Christmas
And fill your heart with cheer;
God grant you health and happiness
Throughout the coming year.
God guide you with his wisdom
And keep you in his care;
This is our special wish for you—
This is our Christmas prayer.

Author Unknown

18

Let Us Keep Christmas

Whatever else be lost among the years,
Let us keep Christmas still a shining thing:
Whatever doubts assail us, or what fears,
Let us hold close one day, remembering
Its poignant meaning for the hearts of men.
Let us get back our childlike faith again.
                              Grace Noll Crowell

19

My Gift

What can I give him
Poor as I am?
If I were a shepherd,
I would give him a lamb,
If I were a wise man,
I would do my part—
But what can I give him,
Give my heart.
Christina G. Rosetti

Christmas Prayer

Let not our hearts be busy inns,
    That have no room for thee,
But cradles for the living Christ
    And his nativity.

Still driven by a thousand cares
    The pilgrims come and go;
The hurried caravans press on;
    The inns are crowded so!

Here are the rich and busy ones,
    With things that must be sold,
No room for simple things within
    This hostelry of gold.

Yet hunger dwells within these walls,
    These shining walls and bright,
And blindness groping here and there
    Without a ray of light.

Oh, lest we starve, and lest we die,
    In our stupidity,
Come, Holy Child, within and share
    Our hospitality.

Let not our hearts be busy inns,
    That have no room for thee,
But cradles for the living Christ
    And his nativity.
                    Ralph Spaulding Cushman

21

"And the Word Was Made Flesh"

Light looked down and beheld Darkness.
  "Thither will I go," said Light.
Peace looked down and beheld War.
  "Thither will I go," said Peace.
Love looked down and beheld Hatred.
  "Thither will I go," said Love.
  So came Light and shone.
  So came Peace and gave rest.
  So came Love and brought Life.
                    Laurence Housman

22

Christmas Everywhere

Everywhere, everywhere, Christmas tonight!
Christmas in lands of fir tree and pine,
Christmas in lands of the palm tree and vine,
Christmas where snow peaks stand solemn and white,
Christmas where cornfields lie sunny and bright,
  Everywhere, everywhere, Christmas tonight!

Christmas where children are hopeful and gay,
Christmas where old men are patient and gray,
Christmas where peace, like a dove in its flight,
Broods o'er brave men in the thick of the fight.
  Everywhere, everywhere, Christmas tonight!

For the Christ-child who comes is the master of all,
No palace too great and no cottage too small;
The angels who welcome Him sing from the height,
"In the city of David, a King in his might."
  Everywhere, everywhere, Christmas tonight!

Then let every heart keep its Christmas within,
Christ's pity for sorrow, Christ's hatred for sin,
Christ's care for the weakest, Christ's courage for right,
Christ's dread of the darkness, Christ's love of the light,
  Everywhere, everywhere, Christmas tonight!

So the stars of the midnight which compass us round
Shall see a strange glory, and hear a sweet sound,
And cry, "Look! the earth is aflame with delight,
O sons of the morning, rejoice at the sight."
  Everywhere, everywhere, Christmas tonight!

Phillips Brooks

23

The Coming Child

Welcome! all wonders in one sight!
  Eternity shut in a span.
Summer in winter, day in night,
  Heaven in earth, and God in man.
Great little one! whose all-embracing birth
  Lifts earth to heaven, stoops heaven to earth!
Richard Crashaw

24

The Lamb

Little lamb, who made thee?
Dost thou know who made thee,
Gave thee life, and bid thee feed
By the streams and o'er the mead;
Gave thee clothing of delight,
Softest clothing, woolly, bright;
Gave thee such a tender voice,
Making all the vales rejoice?
  Little lamb, who made thee?
  Dost thou know who made thee?

Little lamb, I'll tell thee;
Little lamb, I'll tell thee.
He is called by thy name,
For he calls himself a lamb;
He is meek and he is mild,
He became a little child.
I a child, and thou a lamb,
We are called by his name.
  Little lamb, God bless thee!
  Little lamb, God bless thee!
                    William Blake

25

Before the Paling of the Stars

Before the paling of the stars,
  Before the winter morn,
Before the earliest cockcrow,
  Jesus Christ was born:
Born in a stable,
  Cradled in a manger,
In the world his hands had made
  Born a stranger.

Priest and king lay fast asleep
  In Jerusalem,
Young and old lay fast asleep
  In crowded Bethlehem;
Saint and angel, ox and ass,
  Kept a watch together
Before the Christmas daybreak
  In the winter weather.

Jesus on his mother's breast
  In the stable cold,
Spotless Lamb of God was he,
  Shepherd of the fold:
Let us kneel with Mary maid,
  With Joseph bent and hoary,
With saint and angel, ox and ass,
  To hail the King of Glory.
                    Christina G. Rossetti

The Word
John 1:1–5

In the beginning was the Word,
  And the Word was with God,
  And the Word was God.
He was in the beginning with God.

All things came
  Through him;
  And apart from him
Came not a thing which has come.

In him was life;
  And the life was the light of men.
And the light shines in the darkness:
  And the darkness has not overcome it.
      The Bible in Modern English, 1909

27

Quatrain

Here is the truth in a little creed,
  Enough for all the roads we go:
In love is all the law we need,
  In Christ is all the God we know.
                    Edwin Markham

28

Incarnate Love

Love came down at Christmas,
  Love all lovely, love divine;
Love was born at Christmas,
  Star and angels gave the sign.

Worship we the godhead,
  Love incarnate, love divine;
Worship we our Jesus:
  But wherewith for sacred sign?

Love shall be our token,
  Love be yours and love be mine,
Love to God and all men,
  Love for plea and gift and sign.
                    Christina G. Rossetti

29

Childhood

To be himself a star most bright
To bring the wise men to his sight,
To be himself a voice most sweet
To call the shepherds to his feet,
To be a child—it was his will,
That folk like us might find him still.

John Erskine

30

The Shepherd Speaks

Out of the midnight sky a great dawn broke,
And a voice singing flooded us with song.
In David's city was he born, it sang,
A Savior, Christ the Lord. Then while I sat
Shivering with the thrill of that great cry,
A mighty choir a thousandfold more sweet
Suddenly sang, Glory to God, and Peace—
Peace on earth; my heart, almost unnerved.
By that swift loveliness, would hardly beat.
Speechless we waited till the accustomed night
Gave us no promise of sweet surprise;
Then scrambling to our feet, without a word
We started through the fields to find the Child.

John Erskine

31

In Thine Own Heart

Though Christ a thousand times
  In Bethlehem be born,
If he's not born in thee
  Thy soul is still forlorn.
The cross on Golgotha
  Will never save thy soul,
The cross in thine own heart
  Alone can make thee whole.
                    From the German of
                      Angelus Silesius

32

Christmas Joy

Somehow, not only for Christmas,
But all the long year through,
The joy that you give to others
Is the joy that comes back to you;

And the more you spend in blessing
The poor and lonely and sad,
The more of your heart's possessing
Returns to make you glad.

John Greenleaf Whittier

A Christmas Acrostic

C is for the Christ Child
who in a manger lay.

H is for the Heavenly Hosts
who sang that happy day.

R is for rejoicing
at the Savior's birth.

I is for incense, gold, and myrrh,
the Magi's gifts of worth.

S is for the Shepherds
who heard the angels sing.

T is for the tidings
the messengers did bring.

M is for the manger
the Christ Child's cradle.

A is for the animals
who shared the humble stable.

S is for the star seen in the sky that day
which led the wise men to the place where Jesus lay.

A Christmas Wish

H earts filled with joy

A mazement, adoration,

P eace,

P lenty, and

Y outhful imagination.

C hrist in your Christmas;

H ope in your heart

R ighteousness,

I mmortality,

S erenity of mind,

T ime for the good things,

M usic and rhyme,

A bsence from strife,

S alvation from sin, and Christ's Spirit within.

Christ in Christmas

C   hrist, the only begotten Son of God, looked at the sinful world and realized its need for

H   elp. In council with the Father it was agreed that he would give up his high and exalted place and bring to sinful men

R   edemption. He would go to earth in person and through the miracle of birth would become the

I   ncarnation of God in human flesh. He would be born of a virgin with God as his Father, and enter into the sinful world as its

S   avior. His holiness, his exemplary life, his sinlessness, his plan of redemption, his death, and his resurrection would bring to earth the great

T   ransformation needed by all mankind. So he came, as decided in the councils of eternity, and through his coming he brought the

M   elody of heaven to earth. A babe in swaddling clothes, divine, whose birth was announced by the singing of angels on high was to bring

A   ssurance to all mankind that God cared enough to send his only begotten Son that all who believe in him might have

S   alvation and eternal life. Only through personal acceptance of him, God's great gift to man, can there be real Christmas in the human heart.